Lion of Light

The Spiritual Life of Madame Blavatsky

Gordon Strong

Lion of Light

The Spiritual Life of Madame Blavatsky

Gordon Strong

AXIS MUNDI
BOOKS

Winchester, UK
Washington, USA

First published by Axis Mundi Books, 2013
Axis Mundi Books is an imprint of John Hunt Publishing Ltd., Laurel House, Station Approach,
Alresford, Hants, SO24 9JH, UK
office1@jhpbooks.net
www.johnhuntpublishing.com
www.axismundi-books.com

For distributor details and how to order please visit the 'Ordering' section on our website.

Text copyright: Gordon Strong 2013

ISBN: 978 1 78099 653 0

A CIP catalogue record for this book is available from the British Library.

Design: Lee Nash

Printed in the USA by Edwards Brothers Malloy

We operate a distinctive and ethical publishing philosophy in all
areas of our business, from our global network of authors to
production and worldwide distribution.

CONTENTS

Books by Gordon Strong

Stanton Drew and its Ancient Stone Circles
King Arthur, The Waste Land and The New Age
Merlin – Master of Magick
Tarot Unveiled
Sun God and Moon Maiden – The Secret World of The Holy Grail
Brides Mound – Gateway to Avalon
Dawn of The Goddess

Faith is believing in what you know ain't so.
Mark Twain

...but more beautiful still was the world of my wishful thinking,
richer still the play of my waking dreams. Reality was never enough,
there was need of magic.
Herman Hesse

When I have fears that I may cease to be
Before my pen has glean'd my teeming brain...
John Keats

Acknowledgements

Jenny Dix, Secretary of the Bristol Theosophical Society, could not have been more helpful in allowing me access to the library at the Bristol Lodge.

Alan Richardson suggested an approach to the subject that was incisive, and also provided me with some valuable material.

David Matthews offered some excellent information on Blavatsky's nativity.

Jane Marshall, and Victoria Brudal, loaned me books and provided much encouragement.

Introduction

In any age, Helena Petrovna Blavatsky, or *Madame Blavatsky*, as she is usually known, would have been a phenomenon. She possessed the kind of majestic personality which, with consummate ease, dwarfs ordinary folk. Her life was an extraordinary enigma, and as myth breeds other myths, there are not a few surrounding Blavatsky. She has been vilified and championed in equal measure, and it is a struggle to arrive at any balanced view of her achievements, or her shortcomings. What is certain, however, is that she was a courageous and pioneering woman who, largely by her own efforts, established 'spirituality' as an ethos. She also taught that the soul – the 'Inner World' – of any individual, is a place not to be feared, but cherished.

Inevitably, much has been written about Blavatsky, both during her life and after her death. In the 1990s, eighteen separate biographies in English existed, and the number must inevitably now be greater. Some of these accounts seek to paint a flawless picture of their subject; others attempt to vindicate what are seen as misdemeanors, while a few are openly hostile.

This writer has no literary axe to grind; the motive for embarking on such a study being a fascination and respect for the subject, that, and his own continuing involvement with the metaphysical in all its many guises. Of the latter, the presence of Blavatsky has been most marked whilst the book was being written, and the author trusts that his subject approves of what has been said about her. Knowing now a little of her character, he feels certain that Blavatsky will inform him, and most forcibly, if she does not.

Madame Blavatsky was a remarkable woman, and we owe her a great deal. A singular, driven individual, she saw her mission as being to inform and enlighten the world. These are high ideals, and her reward has not been equal to her efforts.

Blavatsky deserves to be given due recognition as one of the most significant figures in the esoteric milieu. She knew only too well that far-reaching changes were coming to the world in the twentieth century. Her beliefs and her vision are even more relevant now in the twenty-first century than when she first voiced them.

Gordon Strong
November 2009

Early Days and Early Travels

I cannot forecast to you the action of Russia. It is like a riddle wrapped in a mystery inside an enigma.
Winston Churchill

A cholera plague raged through Europe on the night that Elena Petrovna Hahn was born. At her baptism, the robes of the hastily summoned priest caught fire. Such was the auspicious beginning to the life of one of the most extraordinary characters of the nineteenth century, one whose influence would last much longer than her comparatively short sojourn upon this Earth. The heavens chose 12th of August 1831 for her birth, in Ekaterinoslav, a district of the Ukraine, then part of the Russian Empire. She was the child of a Colonel in the Russian Army, Peter Von Hahn, and his wife, Helena Andreyevna. The name Hahn is a patronymic form of *Johannes* and derives from *hane*, high German for 'rooster'. The symbolism of this creature is of conceit, and sexual activity – both qualities that would later be attributed to our subject, and not always fairly.

Her mother claimed the lineage of one of the oldest Empire families, a direct descendant, she said, of Grand Duke Rurik, the first ruler of Russia. It was perhaps inevitable that her mother should be a novelist, and Helena's sister Vera, also wrote occult fiction. The education of Helena, as she was soon to be called, came to be supervised by her maternal grandmother. This lady was a princess, her husband, the governor of Saratov. Of Helena's other relations, most prominent was her first cousin Sergei Witte, who later became prime minister of Russia in the reign of Tsar Nicholas II.

Inevitably, such a privileged background would do much to

3

determine the kind of childhood Helena would enjoy. What made this little girl different from her peers was the strength of her 'inner life'. This quality would ensure that she would never be just a conventional member of the elite in Russian society, and her contacts with the 'other side' also made her both sensitive and wilful. Much that terrified her as a child was propagated by her own imagination, and in later years her often morbid sensibility led to an inability to accept criticism, or even what might be termed 'sensible advice.' She was idealistic, naïve and often unworldly. That said, she commanded respect, and considering her capricious temperament, a great many people throughout her life were completely devoted to her. Few recollections exist of Helena's childhood, but this, from the pen of an unnamed aunt, is revealing:

> She was...very lively and highly gifted, full of humour, and most remarkably daring; she struck everyone by her self-willed and determined actions...Her restless and very nervous temperament, one that led her into the most unheard-of ungirlish mischief...her passionate love and curiosity for everything unknown and mysterious, weird and fantastic; and foremost of all, her craving for independence and freedom of action – a craving that nothing and no one could control; all this, combined with an exuberance of imagination and a wonderful sensitiveness, ought to have warned her friends that she was an exceptional creature...

The aunt goes on to tell of Helena's nocturnal conversations with invisible personages, and of her being able to answer questions as if she were a 'sibyl entranced'. Her ability to converse with spirits, whether departed from this world or not, was in evidence from her early childhood. Between nine and sixteen years of age she regularly communicated with the spirit of Tekla Lebendoff, a middle-aged woman, who was very much alive, and lived in

Reval in Estonia. A fuller account of Helena's gifts comes from her sister Vera – later Mme Jelihovsky. The following passage, though lengthy, is worth quoting for the insight that it provides, of a remarkable child:

'...daring and fearless in everything else, she often got scared into fits by her own hallucinations...she would shut her eyes tight during such visions, and run away to hide...screaming desperately and frightening the whole household. At other times she would be seized with fits of laughter, explaining them by the amusing pranks of her invisible companions. She found these in every dark corner, in every bush of the tick park that surrounded our villa during the summer months; while in winter, when all our family emigrated back to town, she seemed to meet them again in the vast reception rooms of the first floor...Helena was found several times during the night hours in those dark apartments in a half-conscious state, sometimes fast asleep, and unable to say how she got there from our common bedroom on the top storey. She disappeared in daytime also. Searched for, called and hunted after, she would be often discovered, with great pains, in the most unfrequented localities; once it was in the dark loft, under the very roof to which she was traced, amid pigeons' nests, and surrounded by hundreds of those birds...At other times...the deserter would be found, after hours of search in deep conversation with seals and stuffed crocodiles...For her all nature seemed animated with a mysterious life of its own. She heard the voice of every object and form, whether organic or inorganic; and claimed consciousness of being...even for inanimate things such as pebbles...[1]

Mysticism came as naturally to Helena as breathing. The perceptions that might take a sage an entire lifetime to acquire, she owned at birth. She also displayed the temperament of the occultist, laying down foundations on the Inner Plane – there for the future. Already she has a sense that time is malleable, perhaps invisible. High magic is being unconsciously embraced, and as Madame Blavatsky, she will later display all the courage and conviction that the practitioner must own in order to perform her miracles. Helena sought out the acquaintance of Baranig Boyrak, an old sage who lived near her grandparents' home. She wished him to teach her the language of insects, birds and animals. Whether he did so is not recorded, but he certainly recognized her as being an exceptional young girl and spoke of her thus:

> This little lady is different from all of you. There are great events lying in wait for her in the future. In thinking that, I will not live to see my predictions (fulfilled); but they will come to pass.[2]

Helena's father was not convinced of her psychic ability until one day when she informed him of the significance of the family name. It came about that during the Crusades, Count Rottenstern von Hahn of Meckelenburg had appended 'Hahn' to the family name, and put a cock's image on his coat of arms. What prompted this move was an incident involving an ancestor at war:

> ...while sleeping in his tent, the Knight Crusader was awakened by the cry of a cock to find himself in time to kill, instead of being stealthily killed by an enemy who had penetrated into his tent...[3]

Blavatsky always maintained that she felt the presence of a strong guardian very early on in her life, and swore that this 'protector' saved her from certain death on several occasions. She describes him as being an Oriental – a tall, white-robed figure. Blavatsky is supposed to have actually encountered him in London in 1851, on a visit to England with her father. The meeting apparently took place in Hyde Park, by the river Serpentine. It has been suggested by astrologers, and with some telling evidence, that the influence of Neptune in Blavatsky's nativity, determined certain aspects of her personality. Neptune bestows imaginative and idealistic qualities, though deception and confusion may at the same time plague the native. Mystical experiences were commonplace in her youth and they somehow formed the rock of her beliefs, and thus her conscious life. This would not have been allowed to happen had she not been surrounded by understanding company; her uniqueness was not stifled but even encouraged. Her mentors were active during a period that has been described as the Russian Enlightenment.

The Russian Empire had actively suppressed Ukrainian culture in the 1860s yet a great upsurge in interest in all things mystical and spiritual sprung up in the following decades, and many artists, writers and thinkers in Russia adopted a metaphysical approach to life. Among these progressive figures in Helena's childhood was Taras Schevchenko, the romantic poet and painter. It is interesting to note that in 1848 he won a Silver Medal for his painting 'The Gypsy Fortune Teller', the same year that Helena's young life dramatically changed. It might be conjectured that Blavatsky was following the zeitgeist, and though she would be parted from her native land for a great part of her life, she retained her Ukrainian spirit.

The Ukraine is the heartland of Russia, and still preserves the grandeur that bestows upon it a singular character. Originally inhabited by peoples known as the Rus', from which the name Russia derives, the soul of the country firmly rests here. In the tenth century, Vladimir, Prince of Kiev was responsible for bringing the Orthodox Greek Christianity to the Ukraine, being informed by his emissaries that its liturgy was more impressive than that of the other faiths. The spiritual roots of the land were part pagan, part Christian and later esoteric. Freemasonry was most fashionable among the aristocracy in the time of Catherine the Great, and its influence brought the enlightenment to Russia. Buddhism too had always hovered in the background, spicing and leavening the doctrinal mix.

In Kiev, the oldest church was dedicated to St. Sophia, part of the Gnostic trinity, adding another dimension. Any assessment of Blavatsky cannot ignore her upbringing and her environment. The former made her autocratic; the latter gave her a singular view of the world. It would be meaningless to make generalisations concerning the Russian temperament, yet a certain melancholy and fatality are always present within it. The teachings and the ambiance of the Russian Orthodox Church may well have influenced Blavatsky as a child, and it may have always had a home deep in her unconscious. To W.B.Yeats she explained, 'The Greek Church, like all true religions, was a triangle, but it spread out and became a bramble bush, and that is the Church of Rome...'[4]

Quite why Helena Hahn agreed, at the age of sixteen, to marry General Nikifor, or Nicephore, Blavatsky, a man many years her senior, has never been made abundantly clear. It has been said that on being told by her governess that, because of her ill-temper, no man would ever marry her, Helena rose to the challenge and forced Blavatsky to propose. If she did so 'for a dare' then Helena displayed those qualities that teenagers always do, namely – pride, recklessness and a bad temper. By even contemplating this bizarre union, she thought she was somehow spiting the world, for often the goal of a truculent adolescent is to shock those around her. Once this was achieved, however, Helena deeply regretted what she had done. The general may have even been in his sixties, which made the prospect even more unpalatable. If she had believed that marriage would somehow bring her a degree of freedom, it was a rash assumption.

That she was not committed to her marriage was proved when she attempted to flee from her husband on the day after they were wed. As it was, she was unwilling to remain in his company for longer than three months, after which she succeeded in leaving him for good. The immediate consequences of that decision are well-documented – the return to her grandfather's house, and his dispatching of his granddaughter back to her father. What happened after that is almost anybody's guess, for this event marked the beginning of the mysteries that were to surround this extraordinary woman throughout her life.

Blavatsky was always a wonderful storyteller. It was never difficult for her to hold an audience in enraptured silence with her tales – and some were taller than others. The biographer must always take into account this fantastic aspect of Blavatsky when he attempts to render a true picture of her life. To approach this extraordinary figure as if she were anything other than extraordinary would be a gross error. The key to understanding Blavatsky is to view her life as two separate, yet entwined, narratives, one 'ordinary' reality, the other totally marvellous. It is as if from the moment she left Russia, she became someone else – the figure that she wished to be – a romantic adventuress. She undoubtedly was that person, and more significantly, she believed she was.

An important magical principle is being demonstrated already in her life, and Blavatsky was certainly capable of performing magic if she wished. If the practitioner believes he is in a certain place, then that is where he is. In her life, Blavatsky adopted a different stance to suit the circumstances that she found herself in, and this chameleon aspect is another key to her personality, as we shall discover. Now, we pass on to that part of Blavatsky's life when the world appears to be at her feet.

In the eighteenth century lived one Lady Hester Stanhope, a legendary traveller in the Middle East. There she was received with great respect by the Turkish and Bedouin Sheiks who ruled that part of the world. She dressed in the costume of a Turkish male, a purple velvet robe, embroidered trousers, turban and slippers. She journeyed to the Muslim city of Damascus where she refused to wear a veil, but such was her formidable personality that she was not censured by the inhabitants. Lady Hester went on to visit the ancient city of Palmyra in Syria, a fabulous place known as the 'Bride of the Desert', and it was here that she began to realise her destiny. Hearing omens from soothsayers and prophets that she was to be the bride of the New Messiah, she settled in her new homeland and was crowned Queen Hester by those who were devoted to her. In command of a court, and renowned for her gifts of divination, she settled and eventually died, in the area now known as the Lebanon. When Blavatsky found fame, and was questioned in interviews about these early years, she was occasionally compared to Lady Hester by journalists desperate for copy.

Towards the end of her life, Blavatsky permitted Alfred Percy Sinnett, known as A.P. Sinnett, to embark upon her biography. A great portion of her life was to remain inviolate she informed him. Sinnett was informed in no uncertain terms that a veil must be drawn over anything that happened to her before the advent of the Theosophical Society in 1875. Blavatsky was adamant:

> ...no one can expect me to stand on Trafalgar Square and to be taking into my confidence all the city roughs and cabmen that pass. And even these have more my respect and confidence than your reading and literary public...[5]

After her death, a steady trickle of reminiscences and recollections of Blavatsky began to emerge. Many of these pieces were trivial or waspish. With the publication of the memoirs of Blavatsky's cousin, Count Serge Witte, something of value came to light for the first time. It is from these pages that we glean the details of her dramatic departure from her husband, and soon afterwards her equally colourful 'elopement' with the captain of an English steamer, *The Commodore*. Blavatsky, after embarking at

Constantinople, is supposed to have joined a circus 'as an equestrienne'.

She apparently succeeded in captivating one member of the audience. Agardi Metrovitch, a Hungarian opera singer proposed marriage to her. It is presumed that Blavatsky conveniently forgot to mention her first husband. The subsequent union with Metrovitch is supposed to have produced a child named Yuri. The truth of this is impossible to ascertain solely from Witte's account. Any knowledge of the death of Metrovich soon afterwards is even more opaque. Did he perish in 1870 from fever, or from the effects of an explosion on board ship in 1871? Witte seems unconcerned about her husband's fate, going on almost in the same breath, to mention that Blavatsky met Daniel Dunglas Home, a celebrated 'conjurer of phantoms' in Paris. It was Home, Witte states, who converted Blavatsky to spiritualism in 1858. She apparently returned to Russia in the same year, and Witte recalls visiting his cousin in a flower shop in Odessa. The only other recollection of Blavatsky, during this period, is from an American artist Albert Leighton Rawson, who is said to have accompanied her on a trip around Cairo in 1850.

As she kept no diary of the period, we have only Blavatsky's word that during the ten years from 1848 and 1858, she visited Egypt, France, Canada, England, South America, Germany, Mexico, Tibet, India and Greece. A suggestion propounded by Kingsland that Blavatsky deliberately falsified the accounts of her travels, to conceal the identity of the places that she visited, is of interest. The notion is supported by accounts of others using similar tactics. Philo, the first-century philosopher, Jacob Bohme, and the Count de Saint-Martin are all said to have engaged in such deliberate deception. Whether or not Blavatsky followed their example, is not known for certain.

It seems that in 1850 she journeyed, with Countess Kisselev, to visit Princess Bagtrion-Muhransky in London, staying in Mivart's Hotel – later Claridges. Blavatsky seems to alternate between travelling alone or, in the early part of her decade of travels, with titled Russian ladies. Mention is made of a pair of these, too discreet to have their full names recorded – only the initials B or C remain to identify them to the cognoscenti. Blavatsky went on to investigate the ruins of the Mayan civilisation at Chicehn-Iza and Uxmal. The often quoted tale that she fought with Garibaldi, and was wounded no less than five times, seems to have a doubtful pedigree. Her excursions into the Near East, to countries such as Syria and the Lebanon, are easier to verify, those being noted by the inhabitants. Further afield in the Levant, her name was mentioned by a merchant in Jiddah to whom she made a present of a ring.

An interesting parallel may be drawn between Blavatsky's travels and those made by Georgio Ivanovich Gurdjieff who, although born some years after Blavatsky, had a remarkably similar life path. Born in the southern parts of the Russian empire, and exposed to the same cultural influences, he is said to have travelled in all the same countries as Blavatsky. Like her, his motive was to discover the truth and wisdom he was certain ancient teachings contained. Similarly, only a vague record of his travels exists. In later years Gurdjieff was subjected to accusations of fraud and espionage, as was Blavatsky. The canon of both their teachings has been subject to suggestions that they are wholly derivative, and arrived in the twentieth century with an ambiguous reputation. With their current re-appraisal, it can be seen that the paradoxes in their individual characters may not always be at odds with a sincere spirituality. It might also be said that Blavatsky in a desire to enlighten humanity tested it to the utmost degree.

During this period, Blavatsky first travelled in North America. She later recalled the Indian tribe near Quebec who stole her fur boots, and her puzzled reaction to the Mormons in Missouri. In New Orleans she investigated voodoo, and from there, travelled through Texas *en route* to Mexico. The Mexican War, the annexation of Texas, and the bitter civil struggles about the issue of slavery would have been raging at the time Blavatsky was travelling in this part of the country. Being surrounded by conflicts and upheaval would always be part of her life.

Her father, having initially given her eighty thousand roubles, received Blavatsky's requests for more funds with laconic resignation. He duly despatched money to any settlement along her way where it was safe to do so. Now financially secure, she travelled in 1852 to Bombay and later to Nepal with the intention of entering Tibet, but did not succeed on this occasion. The following year, 1853, she came to England, but being a Russian she did not receive a warm welcome – it being the eve of the Crimean War. She returned to America, visiting New York, Chicago and San Francisco, remaining there until 1855 when she sailed to Calcutta.

On this occasion she did manage to enter Tibet, albeit in disguise. The Tartar shaman who suggested this ploy was a member of the Kalmuck tribe, a people noted for their liking for making trumpets from the thigh bones of their deceased rulers and high priests. On this expedition Blavatsky not only observed the shaman in the throes of astral travelling, she also sustained her first experience of phenomena. The ethereal form of a woman known to Blavatsky, her physical body three thousand miles away, manifested before her. The shaman achieved this end with the aid of his 'stone' – a carnelian crystal engraved with a sacred triangle.

During this trip Blavatsky is supposed to have ventured into Eastern Tibet – the Khampas – an abode of cutthroats and robbers. Paracelsus, the great figure of magic, also journeyed in the East and, it is said, there he received the Philosopher's Stone. Something of even greater value to Blavatsky's spiritual development was waiting for her in Tibet, though she did not know so at the time. A certain Major Cross, who was the manager of the Dalai Lama's tea estates, later recalled accounts of a white woman who travelled in North West Tibet. If Blavatsky made either of these journeys, none can fault her courage. She could be compared to another intrepid traveller, and student of the occult – Aleister Crowley. As an astrological aside, Crowley was born with his ascendant in Leo, the zodiacal sign occupied by Blavatsky's sun. The lion possesses courage, *in excelcis*, which he draws upon in any situation that he finds himself.

Blavatsky never denies that the 'Masters' – her spiritual guides – may have originated in Egypt rather than Tibet, yet she may well have encountered the Tibetan version, in China. A sacred cave, Rung Jung which did service as a temple, was apparently the 'chief location of lamas' and 'the favourite resort of Mahatmas'. Did Blavatsky embrace Lamaism in Tibet? To a searching enquiry by Arthur Lillie, a vociferous critic, she responded:

> I have lived at different periods in Little Tibet as in Great Tibet...I have stopped in Lamaistic convents! I have visited Tzigadze, the Tdashoo Hlumpo territory...I have visited places never visited by Europeans.[6]

As a child Blavatsky had been in the company of Calmucks, ethnic Buddhists who occupied Astrakhan near Siberia. She visited this area, with her uncle, later stating, 'I knew all about Lamas and Tibetans before I was fifteen.' Support for Blavatsky's claim that she had been initiated into Lamaistic teachings, has been forthcoming from Lama Tashi (1833-1937), and Lama Kazi Dawa-Samdup. Their endorsement of Blavatsky's qualifications resulted from her final work – *The Voice of Silence* – a volume based upon the study of thirty-nine Buddhist precepts. Described by Lama Tashi as 'the only true exposition in English of the Heart Doctrine of Mahayana Buddhism', this holy pair concluded that such a profound insight into their religion must have been gained by a devotee who had studied their faith from an early age.

Another question is: Did Blavatsky visit Shigatse, the second most important city in Tibet? Dr. Franz Hartmann, a companion of Blavatsky when she resided in India in later years, employed clairvoyant methods to prove that she had. A geomancer, astrologer and author of occult works, Hartmann was later to found a German branch of the Theosophical Society. His conviction that Blavatsky had travelled to Shigatse was based on psychometry. The example of this art, skilfully employed by a German 'peasant woman' whom he consulted, convinced Hartmann of the validity of his thesis. Testimonials, of Blavatsky's visit to Tibet made by the Masters also exist, but evidence such as this are part of a bigger question, one that we shall investigate in its appropriate place. Blavatsky's sojourn in that country was still comparatively brief, and in 1858 she left at the behest of her secret guardian, journeying to Java, and thence to Europe.

A single woman travelling on her own in the Far East was certainly not a common occurrence in the middle of the nineteenth century, and there appears to be no accounts of any similar expedition. One reference to a certain Annie Taylor, who ventured into Tibet, much later, at the end of the nineteenth century, is revealing. When faced with the prospect of terrible hardship and possible death, this lady curtly informed a surly native chieftain, "I am English and do not fear for my life."[7] With an obvious change of nationality, we may imagine Blavatsky taking the same tone. Hatred and fear of 'foreigners', the prospect of robbery or murder, these were all very real threats to any traveller in those times, and one can only view with amazement Blavatsky's apparent *sang froid* during the expeditions that she undertook. The conclusion is undeniable – we are dealing with a resourceful and tenacious individual.

When, in 1858, Blavatsky returned to her native Ukraine, scandal followed her like bees about a honey pot. It was rumoured that she had been totally immersed in the low life of several European cities – Berlin, Warsaw and Vienna being specifically mentioned. This was to be Blavatsky's first taste of the kind of innuendo that would plague her for the rest of her life, something that she never quite became immune to. It was also said that she had taken part in the Hungarian Revolution in 1849, and twenty years later she was supposed have been involved in the Polish Revolution! As a kind of respite from all this, and her travels, Blavatsky took up a more settled existence. She remained for the most part in Pskoff with her sister Vera – Mme. De Jelihowsky. However, she was not idle on the Inner Planes – in the next ten years Blavatsky was to hone her psychic skills, particularly her mediumistic powers.

Importantly, she learned to distinguish between passive 'elemental' promptings and genuine contact with persons who had 'passed over to the other side'. The former, she believed, only produced thought forms from the collected unconscious of those present at a séance, while the latter were authentic messages of some value. To her credit, Blavatsky never accepted unconditionally any psychic *communiqués* and was anxious, to the point of paranoia, that she might misinterpret the material that had been transmitted to her. Compare that approach with the numerous mediocre mediums who regurgitate any random nonsense they might hear in their heads! Blavatsky may have acted rashly, or with too much heat, but she was never irresponsible in spiritual matters.

She was preparing herself to receive the teachings that would soon come from the Masters. As any occultist knows, only by extreme concentration can one pass into the astral realms, and once Blavatsky had achieved this, other, greater, skills followed. Blavatsky's powers of visualisation were developing; she found it relatively straightforward to read the thoughts of others, describing the sensation as:

...watching people's thoughts as they evolved out of their heads in spiral luminous smoke, sometimes in jets of what might be taken for some radiant material, and settled in distinct pictures and images around them.[8]

Blavatsky also journeyed into the Caucasus, those parts of Georgia known then as Imeretia and Mingrelia. Spending time in the company of shamans, wizards and soothsayers, she learned from them many secrets. These excursions had the effect of alienating Blavatsky from those of her own class. They felt snubbed, not being able to comprehend why the daughter of a colonel would prefer 'smoky huts' to 'brilliant drawing rooms' and they reacted by making her into a pariah. The cycle of Blavatsky making enemies, for no other reason than being of independent mind and following her star, had begun. The years dragged on, but at last the Master had informed her that she must depart once more upon her travels, and America would be her destination. In the great tradition of the *chela* being given no direction, so that he may find his own way, Blavatsky was setting forth into the unknown. She was unaware that she would meet the individual who would have the most influence on her life. The Divine Powers had assigned other journeys for her in the future, but first she must undertake the voyage to a land where she would establish a platform for her philosophy. She was about to journey to the other side of the world – from Russia to America.

2

The American Colonel

'I'm a poor barbarian that fell down from ...Cossack-land in your civilised country like some ill-shaped (meteorite) from the moon.'
Madame Blavatsky

The number of immigrants into America increased greatly in the latter years of the nineteenth century. Particularly, the country was attractive to those from Russia and Poland. Between 1860 and 1914, two million of the inhabitants of these two countries passed into America. The 1870s was a peak time for the voyages that brought eager individuals to the New World, and Blavatsky was one of them. In 1873 she sailed to New York City, and it was to be the place that changed the course of her life. She was forty years of age and had little resources, but more importantly, she had the determination to be a success in her new environment.

Already the decade had not been without incident in America. In 1870 the Confederate states were officially dissolved, and the first African-American member of Congress was sworn in – the Republican candidate for Missouri. An upturn in the economy had followed the end of the Civil War, reflected in a massive boom in railroad construction, but by 1873, when Blavatsky arrived in the city, a slump had set in. Several banks had collapsed, and later the stock market was to follow suit. Ulysses S. Grant, sworn in for a second term, was president of a nation still with her lawless element intact. Jesse James had pulled off the first successful train robbery, netting three thousand dollars, and the Indian wars had just begun. The American army had just formally adopted the Colt 45 as a side arm. In another milieu, Mark Twain, a writer with an interest in the metaphysical and a contemporary of Blavatsky, was approaching the peak of his powers.

Blavatsky came to a city that was developing and changing by the day. The Statue of Liberty had not yet been constructed. Manhattan consisted of a pattern of streets, with houses modest in size by today's standards, and expanses of fields. At first this incomer had little money, and lived in lodgings in the poor quarter, working as a flower seller. When her reputation had been established, she lived in an apartment of seven rooms in West Forty-Seventh Street. By no means was Blavatsky an instant success, the fairy tale did not have such an auspicious beginning. Some time would elapse before she could clearly see the role she might play in, what must have seemed to her, an alien society. Thus she experienced mixed fortunes in the first months she was there, but in her industrious manner, she soon set about establishing her reputation as a psychic and a medium.

From the outset Blavatsky attracted the attention of journalists, and she made good copy. In this way, it was perhaps inevitable that she would meet someone who would not only aid her spiritual progress, but dramatically enhance her reputation. Being a Leo, she both attracted attention, and also craved that element in her life – without it she was not content. It was to be another born under the same zodiacal sign that she would meet. The encounter happened after Blavatsky had spent a year in America.

Henry Steel Olcott was a veteran of the Civil War. He had been given the rank of Colonel after hostilities had ceased, and was employed by the government in Washington. After serving in the commission that was investigating the assassination of Abraham Lincoln, in 1868 he became a lawyer in New York. He was forty-two years old when he met Blavatsky, and his autobiography, *Old Diary Leaves* [9], starts with this event, so it can be assumed that he deemed the event to be extremely significant. His described her thus:

This lady has led a very eventful life...the adventures she has encountered, the strange people she has seen, the perils by sea and land...I never met so interesting and...eccentric a character.[10]

In middle age the Colonel was still attractive, with a silver beard framing handsome features. He enjoyed good health, and had much energy, his only physical defect being 'a lazy eye'. In addition to his legal practice, the Colonel wrote accounts of séances for the newspapers. During the latter half of the nineteenth century spiritualism had become incredibly popular in America. It is said that its adherents could be numbered in millions. A fundamental difference does exist between 'spiritism' and 'spiritualism', but the line seems extremely blurred. Spiritists regard reincarnation as a basic tenet of their belief system, but spiritualists do not necessarily do so, though they may. It has to be said that mostly 'spiritualism' in America at this time was almost a form of necromancy, involving a medium who contacted the spirits of the dead and relayed any communications to their living relatives. The practice still continues today, it is played out in numerous Spiritualist Churches in England every week, and a morbid spectacle it is too.

Blavatsky was undoubtedly ambitious, and she began to display that command and obvious charisma that came to her in those first years in America. Countess Wachtmeister, the wife of a Swedish diplomat has left this, her first impression of Blavatsky and an uncritical view, yet it attempts to capture the singular quality that Madame obviously possessed:

Her features were instinct with power, and expressed an innate nobility of character...what chiefly arrested my attention was the steady gaze of her wonderful grey eyes, piercing, yet calm and inscrutable: they shone with a serene light which seemed to penetrate and unveil the secrets of the heart.[11]

It is of no doubt that the Colonel was more than instrumental in introducing Blavatsky into the Spiritualist circles that flourished in New York. He was the key to her subsequent success and, it must be said, satisfied in part her hunger for fame. The profound consequences of their meeting were mutual. The Colonel was on a mission to subject spiritual phenomena to the discipline of a system and, in Blavatsky, he had discovered a medium powerful enough to test his own theories. As soon as the Colonel discovered that Blavatsky was the extraordinary personality that he had suspected she was, they were inseparable.

Of what was in store for the Colonel if he became part of a spiritual team Blavatsky, was absolutely direct. She promised nothing except – in the Churchillian phrase – 'blood, toil, tears and sweat'. Remembering her own trials, she was not slow to mention the 'incarnated Evils and legions of Devils' that would be waiting to test the Colonel's faith. Blavatsky explained that the beginning of any spiritual journey was always the most rigorous; it was at that moment the initiate was most severely tested. Even with these strictures ringing in his head, the Colonel agreed to the arrangement.

On a domestic level, matters were not quite so straightforward for the Colonel, nor could his behaviour be described as virtuous – understandable, possibly. With the advent of Blavatsky in his life, the Colonel effectively abandoned his wife and family and devoted every day of his life to Madame. Mrs. Olcott later re-married, and it is to be hoped happily. To be ousted from the Colonel's affections almost from the moment that Blavatsky arrived in America, must have been a severe blow to her pride.

And how would the discarded spouse have described her rival? She might have agreed with the rather uncharitable description of Blavatsky as graceless – 'a great Russian bear'. At this stage in her life, she had become a formidable figure – physically. She weighed two hundred and thirty pounds. Her weight may be ascribed to a complete lack of any exercise and, in any modern assessment, a less than sensible diet. She had a liking for fatty meats, and breakfasted on buttered eggs. A big woman with broad shoulders and thick hair, her features she herself described as, 'Kalmuco-Buddhisto-Tartaric', and she possessed conspicuously large eyes that were of an extraordinary blue.

Described variously as 'voluptuous' and 'sensuous', she had too an elegant dress sense that bordered on the theatrical. She favoured hats with plumes, satin tops with much trimming, diamonds and rings, the latter adornment being worn by the dozen. She was always enveloped in a cloud of exotic scent, and wore upon her bosom 'the mystic-jewelled emblem of an Eastern Brotherhood'. If encountered, any temptation to treat this apparition as a figure of fun was not wise – before the stern eye of Blavatsky all quailed. Madame would accept nothing less than devotion from the company that surrounded her. Blavatsky as a sun about which her satellites revolved, was the template that was to be established, and one that from this moment on would not change. She was well aware of the world she had embraced, and Blavatsky had this to say of this milieu, a view part practical and part metaphysical:

> ...the United States are...the most prolific hotbed for mediums and sensitives of all kinds, genuine and artificial – the more I see the danger humanity is surrounded with. Poets speak of the thin partition between this world and the other. They are blind: there is no partition at all...[12]

This is the voice of one who is only too familiar with other planes of existence, one who has travelled in other worlds and does so with consummate ease. Blavatsky was only just beginning to realise the extent of her powers, she had mastered the material and the ethereal world so that they were, to her, as one. The proof is in the various phenomena that she was capable of producing at this time. To summarise these talents – Blavatsky seems to have had the ability to transfer objects from one place to another, to make letters and numbers appear on surfaces, and perhaps most remarkable of all, to produce an exact copy of an object that was indistinguishable from the original. That these exercises of her abilities were greeted with astonishment is hardly surprising.

Blavatsky realised that such exhibitions were necessary to increase her reputation, and so she set about demonstrating them. Unfortunately, apart from awe, other reactions came from her audiences. Those who disbelieved, dismissing such manifestations as merely elaborate conjuring, considered they had the advantage over her because what was happening could only be 'unreasonable'. She was 'damned if she did and damned if she didn't'. The very wonders that she produced were used as a stick to beat her, 'proof' that she must be a charlatan and a fraud.

When she grew relatively prosperous, the 'hangers-on' strove to take advantage of her, and because Blavatsky was generous and hospitable some inevitably did. Those individuals who are aware to an extraordinary degree are sometimes blind to the most obvious, and Blavatsky was one who owned that weakness. Through harsh experience she learned a little on this score, but this trait eventually led to her undoing. She reacted also by taking a too 'black and white' approach to others, and this made her relationships difficult. Being an aristocrat, she decided instinctively and immediately what was important and what was not. She was also unconventional, and the two together produced a disdain for the genteel and the bourgeois. Blavatsky swore vehemently when she wished, and equally played the fool when the mood took her. She criticised anything and everything if she felt it needed to be, and never subtly. Shocking she may certainly have been to those who she did not care if she offended, to others she seemed as a goddess from afar. Blavatsky was now centre stage in New York spiritual circles, and scene was being set for the next part of the drama. The Colonel would refer to it as, 'The Miracle Club' – it was later to be called the Theosophical Society.

3

The Theosophical Society

The word which shall come to save the world shall be uttered by a woman...
Hers is the light of the heavens and brightest planet of the whole seven.
She is the fourth dimension; And her kingdom cometh; the day of the exultation of women.
And her reign shall be greater than the reign of men.
Anna Kingsford

From 1860 onwards, it was evident that a growing interest in spiritual matters had increased markedly in the West. Such a desire resulted in the forming of fraternities with a transcendent principle at their centre. Some provision for those with such an interest already existed – Freemasonry, an organisation founded in the early eighteenth century, was for many their first port of call. Several new Masonic lodges were formed, a great number in America.

When the Theosophical Society was founded in 1875, it was attractive to those who welcomed an alternative to fundamentalist religion and materialist science. The notion of an ancient and secret tradition, personified by spiritual beings, appealed to those who considered man was approaching a new phase of his development. To those who felt part of a modern-thinking society, a brotherly, humane approach to life seemed a refreshing departure from Victorian stuffiness. Most importantly of all, unlike the Masonic lodges, the Theosophical Society welcomed both men and women.

The Oxford English Dictionary – that arbiter of meaning in the civilised world – gives – 'Theosophy. *n.* Any of various ancient

25

& modern philosophies professing to attain to a knowledge of God by spiritual ecstasy, direct intuition, or special individual relations.' The word derives from *Theo Sophia* –'wise of God' in a literal sense. The term is certainly not unique to the Theosophical Society, or indeed to Blavatsky. Derived from the debates held by the scholars of ancient Greece, it was revived in the seventeenth century when speculation upon the true nature of God was rife. It seems that sacred books and mystical traditions had found favour once more among the intelligentsia, and these formed the foundations of the new philosophy.

Henry Steel Olcott – The colonel – was the first president of the Theosophical Society. It was the funds in his bank account that supported the Theosophical Society in the early years. He began his Inaugural Address to the Society with these words:

> In future times, when the impartial historian shall write an account of the progress of religious ideas in the present century, the formation of this Theosophical Society, whose first meeting under its formal declaration of principles we are now attending, will not pass unnoticed.[13]

What might be these principles that were mentioned? Certain clues are there to be read. A catalyst to the forming of the society was a lecture given by New Yorker George H. Felt in the summer of the same year the Society was formed. Felt, an amateur Egyptologist, claimed to be able to evoke the Elements using the methods developed by the old Egyptian priests. He then invited 'persons of the right sort'[14] to test these results by scientific means. What is relevant here is that this approach is at one with the Colonel's original initiative for the Theosophical Society – that of combining the spiritual and the scientific. That notion was the bedrock on which the Theosophical Society was built and it explains, to some degree, why the Society rejected certain beliefs and welcomed others. As soon as Blavatsky became the Society's icon its principles were those of its leader.

Theosophy is a concept almost as infinite as God himself, it is hardly surprising that it has spawned a multitude of interpretations. Blavatsky preferred the name 'Divine Wisdom', so as to distance the Society and its philosophy from any Judaic reference. She often refers to 'gods' in her writings more often than not a reference to the pantheon of deities that make up the Hindu faith, and to a lesser degree Tibetan Buddhism. Blavatsky's 'The Key to Theosophy' refers, in its copious footnotes, to the 'Eclectic Theosophy' of the Greeks, their own attempt to link the schools of belief then in existence.

The existence of a supreme essence, The Universal Soul, and man's eternal and immortal nature, are its hallmarks. To Blavatsky, the 'Masters', and the sentiments that they communicated to her was immutable proof of the supremacy of this view. 'The Key to Theosophy' is set out in a 'question and answer' format – with exchanges between Blavatsky and her Amanuensis. The work appeared at a late stage in Blavatsky's life, when she had become autocratic to a marked degree, and within its pages any criticisms of her philosophy are simply demolished. It is democracy without room for dissension.

Blavatsky was always at great pains to distance herself and Theosophy from 'Spiritualism', which she came to regard as no better than necromancy, and any tradition of magic that originated in the West. Her intense desire to reduce Western esotericism to a pale shadow of its Eastern equivalent meant that she went to great pains to demonstrate that a Western tradition did not exist – all originated in the East. Blavatsky even attempts to assert that the Qabalah had its origins elsewhere. Such a view is blatantly nonsense, symptomatic of the gross generalisations that Blavatsky was quite capable of making. Once she had set herself on pursuing an end, nothing would stop her, and this trait in her character although laudable in some situations, made her almost incapable of participating in any intellectual debate.

A great fear of being involved herself, or being seen to embrace any practice that might be interpreted as 'black magic', seems to account for her outright dismissal of the occult. Blavatsky's anxiety transposed into an outright prejudice towards Western spirituality, and this prejudice became part of the ethos of Theosophy. It also led Blavatsky, later in her life, to behave in a reprehensible manner towards Mabel Collins, the English author of supernatural tales. Blavatsky's attitude to mysticism is also ambivalent. Hers is an idiosyncratic version of the concept, and one that would probably not be accepted either by a Christian mystic, or even his Eastern equivalent. Theosophy, during Blavatsky's tenure had an approach to spirituality that centred entirely on her own views. This was already being challenged towards the end of her life, and years later the Society altered its *modus operandi* to a degree that Blavatsky would have hardly recognised. Change is inevitable, yet it is remarkable that unity could not be sustained within the Society from the beginning of the twentieth century onwards.

Blavatsky was the forerunner of Joseph Campbell, a twentieth-century philosopher best known for his research into myth. His belief was that spirituality is a search for the fundamental source of all existence, and this force is 'unknown' because it once existed in an undefined state. Campbell considered that all religions were simply 'masks' of the same transcendental truth. Blavatsky would have endorsed the view of the *Rig Veda*, as Campbell did, 'Truth is one, the sages speak of it by many names'. Campbell's conviction that myth was dependent upon faith and imagination in order to exist, led him to the following conclusions:

Whenever the poetry of myth is interpreted as biography, history or science, it is killed. The living images become only remote facts of a distant time or sky. Furthermore, it is never difficult to demonstrate that as science and history, mythology is absurd. When a civilisation begins to reinterpret its mythology in this way, the life goes out of it, temples become museums, and the link between the two perspectives becomes dissolved.[15]

Blavatsky was also convinced that the ancient system of initiation still held good, and that the true teachings were never disseminated by priests. The 'genuinely enlightened', rather than those with an assumed authority, should be the guardians of the mysteries. The masses, from whom she believed the bulk of her disciples would eventually emerge, should be given simple rules to obey. Only when one was a true disciple did the 'real truth' emerge. The Theosophical Society maintained that no religion held the monopoly on truth, and Christianity particularly had failed to provide the world, thus its mission was to provide a universal ethos for the world. Blavatsky cited Christianity as an example of a religion the principles of which were gradually perverted, maintaining that the Gnostics were the only possessors of the true doctrine. Such a view which would certainly be upheld by many who are familiar with the creed of the Templars or the Cathars, both sects having once been regarded as heretical by the established Church.

The notion that 'the infinite cannot be known by the finite' is a basic precept of enlightenment both in the East and the West; hence a minority only comprehends the 'real truth'. It is interesting that the term 'Occult science' has been frequently used to describe Theosophy – the term is not quite as paradoxical as it first might appear to be. To the Colonel and Blavatsky, how much 'truth' a religion possessed was the litmus test of its validity. As Blavatsky's leanings were towards the Eastern tradition, it was inevitable that the Theosophical Society would establish links with that part of the world, specifically India and perhaps even more significantly Ceylon. In her search for the elusive 'truth' Blavatsky was drawn eventually to Buddhism and it is essential that we understand her singular approach to that faith.

Blavatsky insisted that there was a difference between the esoteric and the exoteric, and to her, this was particularly marked in Buddhism. She was a devotee of *Mahayana*, the essential teachings of Buddha, which Blavatsky considered even transcended the 'religion' of Buddhism altogether, because it was the Eternal Truth. Despite her preference for Mahayana, Blavatsky maintained that in an order of 'validity' Buddhism had to be considered on a higher plane than other faiths. In Victorian society, such a view would have been seen as encouraging heathenism, and it is little wonder that the Theosophical Society received such hostility from the Christian Missionary Councils when it began to establish itself in India.

In Blavatsky's time, Eastern thought was unfamiliar, if not totally alien, in the West. Concepts such as all the world being *maya* – illusion – was, far beyond the understanding of the majority. To propose, as Blavatsky did, that the world was dreamed by a cosmic consciousness, and that the material world is merely a reflection of the Eternal Reality – would have been incomprehensible. Regarding reincarnation, Blavatsky proposes a difference between 'memory' and 'reminiscence'. The latter Theosophists regard as being 'the memory of the soul'. Blavatsky talks at great length of the 'Spiritual Ego', a continuing essence of each individual through their chain of incarnations. Theosophy insists this is not the 'Higher Self' of an individual, this 'continuing self' is one every individual possesses. It is not affected by, or reflects the self that occupies the material plane – the incarnated personality.

To the Theosophist, karma operates upon the present incarnation. It is the reason why the distribution of wealth, happiness or suffering seems random, in that the deserving do not always receive their just rewards, and the sinner appears to live in splendour. Such a condition in the world is explained as being yet more evidence of *Maya*. Blavatsky also maintains that Western spirituality confuses a genuine Nirvana with that of a sensual paradise, and commensurably supports the existence of a demon-infested hell. Theosophy did a great service in questioning the notion of duality, but Blavatsky conveniently ignores the metaphysical belief, held for centuries, of the existence of a magical polarity – the union of opposites.

From the fruit of his own studies the Colonel wrote *Buddhist Catechism* [16], a 'rational' view of the faith, still a key text in the understanding of Buddhism. The author makes a genuine attempt to synthesise Eastern and Western thinking, his approach not the same as Blavatsky, more akin to the manner that Jung would also attempt. Blavatsky presents her doctrine as scientific fact, using the same terms as an observation that the planets revolve around the sun. Such an approach is in evidence when the difference between 'soul' and 'mind', even 'spirit' and 'body' is debated. The Greek philosophers had much to say concerning these matters, yet Blavatsky accuses them of gross errors simply because their ideas are not in accord with her thesis. Such an approach does not endear those of a reasoning mind. By analysing and improving an existing philosophy, each age considers it presents a more cogent argument. Blavatsky sets herself against minds greater than her own with supreme conviction but little firepower in her intellectual armoury.

Theosophy stressed the notion that true knowledge results from a unified bond between peoples, thus Blavatsky stressed the need for Theosophists to act in a manner akin to the beliefs of the Society. It may be that the spiritual upsurge in the 1870s may have had a darker outcome in paving the way for the Russian revolution. In a more positive vein, this striving for a 'universal brotherhood' links Blavatsky with the ideals of the 1960s and subsequently the 'New Age'. Theosophy promoted the ideal of equality in society, though the means that were advocated to achieve this end seem to be a little vague. Despite Blavatsky's advocating the re-education of society on broad 'socialistic' principles, history has shown that co-operation between peoples rarely occurs for purely altruistic reasons. Her view that education should centre upon the acquisition of wisdom, and the development of the individual in a homeopathic approach, were ideas later taken up by Rudolf Steiner, for a time responsible for the branch of the Theosophical Society in Germany.

Within the pages of *The Key to Theosophy* Blavatsky takes on those who are hostile towards the Society, and having the consummate riposte – either the critic's words are not worthy of consideration, or they are an ex-member who mistakenly believes they have been wronged. Blavatsky assumes the pose of martyr herself, detailing her suffering and claiming her motive has never been self-gratification. Blavatsky's stating that the Society was so radical in its approach to spirituality that it inevitably aroused fear and hostility, is partly true. It was within the *zeitgeist* to question existing doctrine, and the Theosophical Society was most certainly a catalyst for change. As Joseph Campbell was to remark some years later:

> Man's mental and psychic growth will proceed in harmony with his moral improvement, while his material surroundings will reflect the peace and fraternal good-will which will reign in his mind, instead of the discord and strife which is every-where apparent today.[17]

Blavatsky's vision of the Theosophical Society as a haven of peace and enlightenment was not to become a reality. Rather, it became a political forum within the occult world. A mere eight years after the Society's inauguration the London Lodge was in an uproar, its officers locked in a seemingly irreconcilable dispute over the meaning of 'Theosophy'. Blavatsky would involve herself only marginally in these disputes, and contented herself in her final years with forming an inner circle of a dozen members, the 'Esoteric Group', to have about her. She had, however, not been slow in finding the person who she regarded as her successor. Although Annie Besant would not become president of the Theosophical Society until 1907, twenty-five years earlier Blavatsky had written very positively of a:

> ...lady orator, of deservedly great fame, both for eloquence and learning – the good Mrs. Besant – without believing in controlling spirits, or, for that matter, in her own spirit, yet speaks and writes such sensible and wise things, that we might almost say that one of her speeches or chapters contains more matter to benefit humanity, than would equip a modern trance-speaker for an entire oratorical career.[18]

Annie Besant was a social reformer who embraced the causes of Women's Rights and Irish Home Rule. She was a socialist and later a Marxist, being strongly involved in the Match Girls' Strike of 1888. She turned Theosophist after meeting Blavatsky and became part of her Inner Circle, but this did not prevent her at that time from embracing Freemasonry also. In her characteristic fashion she founded the first Lodge of International Mixed Masonry, *Le Droite Humain.* Her commitment to Freemasonry, like everything else she was involved with, was intense and vigilant. She was instrumental in forming lodges of *Le Droite Humain* all over the world, and held the rank of Most Puissant Grand Commander.

Eventually abandoning her political beliefs entirely, she next took over the presidency of the Theosophical Society. During her considerable time in office, various episodes occurred, the most notorious centring about Charles Webster Leadbeater who she had met in 1894. They were inseparable from that time on, and one is left to marvel at the nature of Besant's personal relationships, which never seemed to be far from conflict and calumny. Leadbeater's career as a Theosophist is shrouded in a clammy cloud of darkness. A self-promoted idea that he was a medium of great repute must be tempered by an infamous tendency not to tell the truth. His claim to have been Blavatsky's pupil, which he was not, must be one of his milder fabrications. Blavatsky first met Leadbeater in 1884. He was then a member of the clergy, continuing to hold holy orders throughout his life. Together they travelled to Colombo where Leadbeater converted to Buddhism. Naturally, a sensation was caused by his decision as this was the first time ever an ordained clergyman had declared himself to be a follower of the Buddha.

Of his subsequent behaviour, the worst example must be Leadbeater's undoubted pederasty, which he indulged in with pupils in his care. This culminated in him being at the centre of a particularly revolting sexual scandal involving these very charges. Having for an extraordinarily long period successfully survived the attacks of his accusers in the Theosophical Society, enough was enough, and he was forced to resign from the Society in 1906. Besant's loyalty to Leadbeater and one can only assume, the latter's total domination of her, was instrumental in him being reinstated in 1908. The move caused a schism in the Society, over one hundred and fifty members resigning from the Society.

The next year, Besant and Leadbeater were also involved in perhaps a more salubrious, but none the less just as far-reaching event. Shortly before Blavatsky died, she had informed her students that the World teacher would soon appear on the planet. The welcoming into this world of a 'new messiah', though the Theosophists would never have dared to publicly employ such a term, was intrinsic to Theosophical beliefs. At least they were close to Blavatsky's heart, she believing this 'coming' would occur in her lifetime. In 1896, her prediction was publicly announced and thirteen years later, Leadbeater met Jiddu Krisnamurti a Hindi boy of fourteen years old, who had arrived with his family at Aydar seeking employment. Leadbeater supposedly recognised the boy's aura as being that of one who has a highly developed spiritual presence. He convinced Besant this was the great 'World teacher' for whom mankind had been awaiting. Krishnamurti's physical appearance was not prepossessing:

> ...apart from his wonderful eyes...he was undernourished, scrawny and dirty; his ribs showed through his skin and he had a persistent cough; his teeth were crooked...moreover his vacant expression gave him a moronic look...[19]

After a legal dispute with Krishnamurti's father, who had sued the Theosophical Society on some unclear pretext, Annie Besant secured custody of the boy and his brother. Besant may have been a surrogate mother for Krishnamurti, who seemed not have involved in any sexual relationship during his lifetime.

A religious brotherhood, the *Order of the Star in the East* was formed, specifically to be led by Krishnamurti. Always a strong-willed personality, hints of such a trait being observed in his adolescence, Krishnamurti proved to be his own man. Without warning, he publicly disowned the order in 1929. He rejected Leadbeater and Besant and saw to it that the substantial donations made to the order would be returned to the donors. It seems that this was not executed quite as promptly as Krishnamurti intended, and the legal entanglements that resulted were not resolved until after his death. The once titled 'saviour' continued to lecture and write of his philosophy, although he espoused no fixed doctrine and insisted that "Truth is a pathless land." Despite his rejection of Theosophy, Besant assigned six acres of land near the Society headquarters as a retreat for the former Messiah, a plot which later became the Krishnamurti Foundation.

In the forty years since the death of Blavatsky, the aims and views of the Theosophical Society had changed so much as to be unrecognisable from Blavatsky and the Colonel's original intentions. A book of instruction from the beginning of the twentieth century[20] illustrates the point. The tone is earnest, and seeks to rationally inform the reader of the irrational. If that appears to be paradoxical, then the Society, from the beginning, has always been so. Its principle of 'Occult Physics' was always built on a quicksand.

However, the book is impressive in the scope of its subject matter. Phenomena such as The Astral Plane, séances, aetheric presences, elementals and angels are summarily dealt with in various articles from different pens, some obviously by Besant and Leadbeater. Much of the material would not be out of place in the manifesto of any spiritual group with spiritual leanings operating in the twentieth century. The book claims that Theosophy will provide answers to any questions about death, manifestations, fears, the soul and other weighty subjects. The banishing of scepticism and superstition is an avowed aim. Concentration, meditation and contemplation are briskly dealt with and heartily recommended to the reader.

Materialisation, including a detailed description of 'precipitation', the method used to explain the appearance of the Mahatma letters, is explained. The colours of the aura are described, along with the nature of telepathy and clairvoyance – with reference to the unconscious. For those wishing to embrace Theosophy, a vegetarian diet is recommended. Basic morality, including telling the truth and not maligning others, is propounded. Spiritual teachers from all major faiths are listed. A plea to study and develop the Inner Life is made; 'All men, irrespective of race, creed, sex, caste or colour, are open windows within themselves...'[21] The only cautionary note that is sounded is against practising magic in any form.

One person who obviously did not heed these dire warnings was a former member of the Society – Dion Fortune. With Aleister Crowley, Fortune must be the paramount figure in the occult world of the twentieth century. She possessed a similar majesty to Blavatsky, and was born in the year before Blavatsky died, which many have seen as significant, in that a magical torch was passed from the one to the other. Fortune always cited the Theosophical Society as being her first port of call when she realised that she was being drawn towards the magical path. Her magical career had already been impressive. Fortune had been initiated into one of the groups that had sprung from out of the ashes of the Golden Dawn, – the London Temple of the Alpha and Omega – in 1919. She had crossed magical swords with Moina Mathers and survived to tell the tale, and was about to form her own school of magic – the celebrated Fraternity of the Inner Light.

With these impeccable references, this formidable figure joined the Christian Mystic Lodge of the Theosophical Society in 1927. She maintained that she did so on instructions from no less than the Master Jesus himself. Did He or she know how short-lived her tenure was to be? From the beginning there was a conflict between her own views and those of the Society. Fortune did not support the Society's alliance with the Liberal Catholic Church, and actively criticised this policy in two publications, namely *The Occult Review* and the Society's own publication, *Transactions*. Those who were behind Leadbeater and Besant could not tolerate such, as they saw it, insubordination.

Fortune, never one to surrender easily when under attack, first spiritedly defended her views. After a time she realised how corrupt the Theosophical Society was and resigned, not only from the Christian Mystical Lodge, but also the Society. Ostensibly, her espousing of the Western Tradition at the expense of the Society's adherence to the Eastern view had caused an irreconcilable problem, but this was not so. Her crime was not to kow-tow to Leadbeater and Annie Besant, who was very much under his influence at this time. Neither did Fortune subscribe to the Krishnamurti Cult which would follow, and was vocal in denouncing Leadbeater and Annie Besant over this issue. She was also to support the 'Back to Blavatsky' campaign that came about some years later.

Before we pass on to examine Blavatsky's beliefs in greater depth, in the media of her writings, it will be instructive to mention one other aspect of the East/West dichotomy with regard to Dion Fortune. In 1919 a dramatic confrontation, on both the material and the Inner planes, occurred between Bomanji Wadia and Fortune. Wadia had originally been a leading light in the Adyar foundation and a great supporter of Krishnamurti. Since that time, Annie Besant had aroused the souls of many Indians in their desire for Indian Nationalism, Wadia being one so affected. He was in England attempting to establish a group, the sole motive of which was to establish the supremacy of the East over the British Empire as it then was.

As would be supposed, Fortune disagreed with this view and Wadia, obviously nettled, resorted to occult methods to frighten her. Dion survived the attack, but it had the effect of embracing the Western Tradition, in the belief that the Eastern path was not for students of magic in the West. She became certain that her own country possessed a serviceable, if not profound, magical tradition and that it should be uppermost in the soul of Britain.

Some well-known figures of the twentieth century, such as Einstein, came under the influence of the Theosophical Society. In literature, W.B.Yeats is the most obvious example, Boris Pasternak, James Joyce and Ezra Pound being perhaps less well known as devotees. In the realm of classical composers Alexander Scriabin admitted to a fascination with Theosophy. More notorious members of the society were Adolf Hitler and Heinrich Himmler. Such an atmosphere of inspiration contrasts unfavourably with the history of the Theosophical Society as one of machinations, intrigues and dissensions.

Of those who, over the decades, were responsible for its business – spiritual or secular – a depressing picture emerges. Yet from within these turgid fogs shines a light – Madame Blavatsky, with the faithful Colonel at her side. It is her own vision and determination that gives the whole movement some meaning.

Blavatsky *is* the Theosophical Society, the 'Back to Blavatsky' movement, although hopelessly nostalgic, demonstrated the power of that influence. As our tale further unfolds we should keep the image of this brave and determined woman, eccentric, irascible, but always focussed ultimately on those higher goals.

4

Writings

*'As for me I write, write, write, as the Wandering Jew walks, walks,
walks, walks.'*
Madame Blavatsky

Apart from founding the Theosophical Society, Blavatsky's
greatest achievement remains in her authorship. What impressions that have been left to us of her formidable persona remain
in those writings. Her two great works, *Isis Unveiled* and *The
Secret Doctrine* continue to sell steadily, and interest in her other
works remains high. As she readily admitted herself, Blavatsky's
formal education was scant. She was no scholar, and had not
written a word of English until 1874, the year following her
arrival in America. Disarmingly, she later confessed, 'I had not
the least idea of literary rules.'[22]

When *Isis Unveiled* came to be written, it was the Colonel who
corrected and revised the text. Ideas, although flowing in a
veritable torrent from her fertile brain, were for her difficult to
organise. It is evident that her books would not have been
published at all if a formidable amount of support had not been
come from a loyal band of disciples and devotees. This is particularly so when *The Secret Doctrine* was being prepared for publication. We owe a great debt those who worked so diligently on
her behalf in the London house at the end of her life.

No evidence that Blavatsky wrote anything before *Isis
Unveiled* has ever been discovered, and it is hard to entertain her
own claim that she wrote articles for Parisian journals before
1874. Sketches and jottings do exist as part of her *oeuvre*, but they
do not give any clue to the character who would later be capable
of writing two highly influential volumes of occult wisdom. In

her 'literary' period, between 1876 and 1890, Blavatsky produced articles, several short esoteric works, and nine occult novels. Of the articles, between fifty or sixty may be viewed on-line. The titles are often fascinating, 'Stray thoughts on Satan', being a good example, and 'The Number Seven in our Society', also promises much. The articles vary in length and, it must be said, in quality. Reading these pieces evokes a suspicion that Blavatsky is often being deliberately disingenuous. When she attempts to make any political comment, even concerning her own homeland of Russia, her grasp of politics is tenuous, to say the least. One article on the plight of the Russian Jews in the nineteenth century displays such a woefully inadequate understanding of the situation that it can hardly be taken seriously.

The seeds of an irritating aspect of Blavatsky's character, a childish assumption that she could never be wrong, were sown early. *The Theosophical Magazine*, to which Blavatsky was a regular contributor, was first published in India in 1879, the annual subscription being six rupees. Towards the end of her life, Blavatsky started another periodical – *Lucifer* – which reflected the views of the Esoteric Lodge she had then inaugurated. The intrigues that surrounded this publication are relevant as they sharply display certain aspects of Blavatsky's character and we shall examine this episode later. Numerous Theosophical magazines have appeared since *Lucifer* and many still continue to be produced.

Throughout her life strange happenings surrounded Blavatsky as clouds clothe the highest mountains. The publication in 1877 of *Isis Unveiled*, Blavatsky's first major work, is no exception. The methods used to put the book together have given rise to much speculation. The character of her publisher, the bizarre Mr. Boston who was actually a bookseller by trade, is equally intriguing. Add to that the reception that the book received, which is also astonishing for several reasons, and the Blavatsky myth ever increases. *Isis Unveiled* took two years to produce, and for an account of its production, we are obliged to rely upon the recollections of the Colonel. The most curious aspect is that Blavatsky insists she was writing facts she did not know, and quoting from works she had never read. In his published recollections, the Colonel describes in some detail how this came about.

According to the Colonel, who occupied the same room, whilst Blavatsky was writing he would observe her pause, more often than not in mid-sentence. She later claimed that at such a moment the very words she needed would appear before her in the air. Echoes of such a procedure can be heard in this account by Frederick Hockley, an occultist of the early nineteenth century:

> I knew a lady who was an admirable seeress, and obtained some splendid answers by means of crystals. The person who has the power of seeing, notices first a kind of mist in the centre of the crystal and the message or answer appears in a kind of printed character. There was no hesitation and she spoke it all off as though she was reading a book, and as soon as she had uttered the words she saw, they melted away and fresh ones took their place.[23]

According to the Colonel, even more remarkable was the manner in which Blavatsky could cause books to materialise upon a shelf. He would obligingly fetch the newly-manifested volume, and from it dictate the piece required, and the book would then disappear. The Colonel insists that he would never have seen the particular book on that shelf before, either before taking it down, or indeed after. As would be expected, help was forthcoming from the 'Masters' who would dictate large parts of text, or alternatively write the manuscript for her while Blavatsky slept. All of this may account for the extraordinary variances in style that the writing displays. The title too gives a clue to Blavatsky's method, in that she is claiming that Isis herself revealed all to her in a constant parade of visions.

Knowing that Blavatsky indulged in drugs at this time, one is tempted to suggest that smoking a little hashish might have induced this panorama of exotic images. On occasion, works of art have been produced while the artist was in state of intoxication. Samuel Taylor Coleridge's *Kubla Khan*, 'a vision in a dream' and stimulated by opium, being the most well-known example. In the twentieth century, the first draft of Jack Kerouac's *On The Road* was supposedly hammered out in three weeks at the typewriter, while the writer was in a haze of amphetamine and marijuana.

By the spring of 1877 Blavatsky's *magnum opus* had grown to half-a-million words. The author was in no mood to edit her material, rather the opposite, continuing to add more and more until the manuscript stood nearly three feet high. Bouton, the publisher, contacted the Colonel and pleaded with him to make Blavatsky desist from increasing the size of the manuscript. The next move by the publisher was to call in a Mr. Alexander Wilder M.D. who had edited several publications for Bouton. Wilder had heard tell of Blavatsky, described to his ears, affectionately perhaps, as 'the rushing Russian' and he had some interest in arcane matters himself.[24] Wilder reported back to Bouton that he considered the manuscript too long. Bouton duly agreed to its publication, on the condition that it was edited, and set Wilder 'to shorten it as much as it would bear'. Wilder duly abridged *Isis Unveiled*, but 'preserve(d) the thought of the author', and 'without marring the work'. Wilder's account of Blavatsky is useful in that it includes a portrait of Madame at this time. The style is ponderous but nevertheless revealing:

> She was tall but not strapping, her countenance bore the marks and exhibited the characteristics of one who had seen much, thought much, travelled much, and experienced much.

Her figure reminded me of the description which Hippocrates has given to the Scyths, the race from which she probably descended…Her appearance was certainly impressive, but in no respect was she coarse, awkward or ill-bred. On the other hand she exhibited culture, familiarity with the manners of the most courtly society and genuine courtesy itself. She expressed her opinions with boldness and decision, but not obtrusively…she knew a vast variety of topics and could discourse freely upon them.[24]

Other than Wilder's, the manuscript passed through several hands along the way. It is perhaps not surprising that parts were lost, quotes misapplied, and other errors made. Bouton's business methods were nothing short of draconian; he had procured the copyright to *Isis Unveiled*, and thereafter refused, even after being approached on several occasions, to transfer the copyright back to its rightful owner. Finally on Sept. 29th. 1877, the two large volumes that made up *Isis Unveiled* appeared. The cover price was $7.50 for two hardback books comprising one thousand and five-hundred pages. Over a hundred years later, the advertisement copy still sounds impressive:

ISIS UNVEILED, a master key to the mysteries of ancient and modern science and theology. By H.P. Blavatsky, Corresponding Secretary of the Theosophical Society.

'Nearly every myth is based on some great truth'[25] wrote Blavatsky in *Isis Unveiled*. The book itself has become part of the Blavatsky myth, and, like some heretofore undiscovered galaxy, it challenges the powers of the observer to describe it. To summarise the contents of such an all-embracing thesis would be an enormous task, it might be easier to specify what has been left out. The themes are multifarious, and with promiscuous enthusiasm, embrace every spiritual tradition. Some are not to

Blavatsky's liking – particularly Christianity. From Vol. II, ironically titled 'The infallibility of Religion', two chapters, chosen from a plethora of emotive titles, present enough evidence to her prejudices – 'Christian Crimes and Heathen Virtues', and 'Lying Catholic Saints'. Playing a tune that will become very familiar, Blavatsky believes that, for the Westerner, the acquiring of any profound transcendental knowledge is impossible:

> ...its acquisition is practically beyond the reach of white-skinned people...the...idiosyncrasies of the Orientals are utterly wanting in them.[26]

That said, Blavatsky's praiseworthy ideal is for the unification of all existing beliefs. She attempts to summarise the essence of the major faiths, and comment upon their worth when compared to her Oriental template. Such an eclectic mix of esoteric knowledge and established doctrine is bound to produce a work that is eclectic in itself. A random sample – Buddhism, Hinduism, the Qabalah, Ancient Egypt, Revelations, Planetary associations, Shiva, Saturn – might give some insight into the vastness of its themes. Blavatsky's other proposition, one dear to the Colonel's heart, is that science and spirituality may be brought together. Her claim that a, 'knowledge of chemistry and physics is displayed by Indian jugglers',[27] sits oddly in the text. To take another example, Blavatsky states that 'metaphysics requires myths, as much as science needs atoms'. Like many of Blavatsky's ideas, it is impressive on first hearing, but the reasoning is neither explained nor sustained. In much of *Isis Unveiled*, arguments often go unsubstantiated, and rely for their existence on mere hectoring.

What was Blavatsky's motive for writing the book? If we consider that it must have been an exceedingly onerous task for anyone writing such a book in an unfamiliar language, the question may not seem so strange. Yet Blavatsky assures us that, for much of the time, her mind and body are possessed by a higher power:

> '...I am perfectly conscious of what my body is saying and doing – or at least its new possessor. I even understand and remember it all so well that afterwards I can repeat it and even write down *his* words...Yet not with my mind but his own, which enwraps my brain like a cloud...'[28]

It cannot be denied that *Isis Unveiled* was a full-blooded, almost desperate attempt to consolidate all the revelations, experiences and half-formed ideas that had been brewing in Blavatsky's mind for over twenty years. It is an outpouring of convictions – sprawling, often difficult to comprehend, but always wholly original. Blavatsky had set herself an almost impossible task of constructing, not only a coherent philosophy, but one that would be spiritual counsel for a future generation. Presenting the world with a true light to guide them was her aim. The reception that followed its appearance was an omen of how the rest of Blavatsky's life would develop. The arrival of *Isis Unveiled* was more dramatic even than the founding of the Theosophical Society, for its publication made her teachings available to a wider audience.

Initially the reviewers were confused, even mildly damning, the only praise coming, surprisingly in that it was a Catholic newssheet, from the *New York Herald*. But, just as quickly the tide turned, and the book began to be described in such terms as, 'this remarkable work will prove of absorbing interest', 'the most remarkable book of the season', 'a mine of curious information', 'an abundance of entertainment'. In the next ten days, the book sold out completely. Blavatsky had triumphed...but not for long. Throughout her life Blavatsky would always have critics, and as the echoes of praise died down, the cries of those determined to denigrate her achievement became more shrill.

Predominant in these vituperations was the rumour that an acquaintance of Blavatsky and the Colonel, one who sat on the Council of the Theosophical Society, was the true author. Joseph Henry Louis Charles, Baron de Palm, Grand Cross Commander of the Sovereign Order of the Holy Sepulchre, Knight of St. John of Malta, Prince of the Roman Empire – that was his illustrious-sounding name. If anyone deserved the title of 'fraud', it was this charmingly mannered, penniless, old nobody. At his death a trunk 'full of manuscripts' had been discovered, and it was implied that within these papers was the entire *corpus* of Blavatsky's work. It was also said that Madame was in a permanent state of terror lest this should be revealed to the public. That there was not a shred of evidence for this assumption seems to have been conveniently forgotten. When the trunk was opened, all that was found was a collection of worthless stocks.

The Spiritualist movement did not find *Isis Unveiled* to their liking, condemning it as wholly plagiarised and the work of the Devil. More serious accusations, not of diabolism but of plagiarism, would emerge later, and we shall not fail to examine them. As we are wholly concerned at this moment with reviewing her writings let us see where Blavatsky's next enthusiasm lay. The artist tends to be dismissive of earlier work and Blavatsky was no exception, later referring to *Isis Unveiled* as 'confused' and 'trash'. Her future dissatisfaction would come from the assessment that her philosophy was not made sufficiently clear in its pages. The Colonel agreed, and thus, almost immediately after *Isis Unveiled* was published, Blavatsky was planning a sequel.

5

India

'Do you think that I would stand going about with that mad Frenchwoman if I did not know what lies behind her.'
Colonel Olcott

We must return to 1878, to discover that by May of that year the membership of the Theosophical Society had dwindled to a few faithful supporters. All that would soon change when Blavatsky embarked on her second great quest, one that would give her a new spiritual direction, and one that would take her on a journey halfway across the world. The Colonel was instrumental in this great change. Through the offices of an old friend, Moolji Thackersey, the Colonel had begun to correspond with a certain Swami Dayanada Sarasvatji.

This imposing figure was the founder of the *Arya Samaj* a devout movement that embraced the pure Vedic faith. The Swami was also anxious that his faith should propagate in the West. In consequence the Theosophical Society changed its name to *The Theosophical Society of the Arya Samaj*. By, it seemed, divine guidance; the Swami's organisation was based in Northern India. This was the abode of the Mahatmas, the 'great souls', those who retain an earthly form in order to help mankind in its spiritual progress. These 'Masters of the Himalayan Brotherhood' were soon to play a great part in the direction that Blavatsky's life was to take. As if strengthening this divine will, the Colonel had experienced an intense vision:

'I saw towering above me in his great stature an Oriental clad in white garments, and wearing a head-cloth or turban of amber-striped fabric, hand-embroidered in yellow floss-silk.

Long raven hair hung from under his turban to the shoulders; his black beard, parted vertically on the chin in the Rajput fashion, was twisted up at the ends and carried over the ears; his eyes were alive with soul-fire; eyes which were at once benignant and piercing in glance; the eyes of a mentor and a judge, but softened by the love of a father who gazed on a son needing counsel. He was so grand a man, so imbued with the majesty of moral strength, so luminously spiritual, so evidently above average humanity, that I felt abashed in his presence, and bowed my head and bent my knee as one does before a god or god-like personage. A hand was lightly laid on my head, a sweet though strong voice bade me be seated, and when I raised my eyes, the presence was seated in the other chair beyond the table.'[29]

The Master, for this was who he was, informed the Colonel that this was a crucial time in his life and also of Blavatsky. Great work awaited them both, and they must be ready to embark on this path at a moment's notice. The Master left his turban, as a sign that he had indeed been in the Colonel's presence and that he was not a figment of the Colonel's imagination. The Colonel was devastated by the experience, and thought long and hard about all this before informing Blavatsky. He knew full well that they had no choice but to make the journey to India, and in doing this they would both be taking a most formidable step.

Blavatsky was forty-seven years old, and not in the best of health, the Colonel was around the same age. He had more to lose, for if he agreed upon this venture he was in effect abandoning completely his wife and three children. It would be a move that would have caused any man, no matter how dedicated he was to the spiritual path, a few qualms. Neither could he or Blavatsky put their hands on any substantial funds. In the event, what money they did take with them to India was gleaned from the sale of the artefacts in the 'Lamasery', the apartment in New York where they had lived together, and where Blavatsky had held court. This, as they expected, amounted to very little. But, with high hopes, they sailed from New York to Liverpool, and after a brief sojourn in London at the Theosophical Society Headquarters, set sail for India, entering Bombay harbour in February 1879.

In order to gain a complete picture of the country, it is necessary to consider the mood of the Indian people at this time. The British Raj had done much to benefit the colony that they ruled, and among these improvements had been the introduction of education. This move had most profoundly affected the generation who had followed those who had known the Indian Mutiny of forty years earlier. With an entirely different outlook, intellectually inspired, even modern in their thinking, this new wave had taken up the cause of Indian Nationalism. Wishing to reclaim their identity, they had sought to reclaim their roots in Ancient India. To them, this was typified by the Vedas, the Sanskrit writings which they saw as reflecting the great glory of their culture. As soon as they arrived in India, Blavatsky and the Colonel were seen to be wholeheartedly embracing these ideals. It was a wholly unexpected reaction on the part of two Westerners, and one which surprised and delighted the Indian populace.

The feast of *Shivaratri* was a dramatic introduction to India for the visitors. They experienced the whole colourful and intense panoply of life on the streets of Bombay. But all was not frenzied excitement, a certain Babu Surdass who insisted that he was one hundred years old, offered Blavatsky and the Colonel his advice. By keeping the mind calm, the soul is untroubled, and perceives only truth. His visual analogy was that the sun can be seen only in water that is smooth. They would need all the tranquillity they could muster as the year came to an end. Enmity, the dark cloud that seemed to dog Blavatsky all her life, appeared on the horizon.

It came in the form of the Christian missionaries who, naturally enough, regarded the pair with suspicion. This emotion they might well have dismissed had it not turned into outright hostility. Attacks on the Theosophical Society, and personal vicissitudes against the Colonel and Blavatsky began to appear in the British press in the first months of 1881. The Saturday Review described the pair as, 'a couple of unscrupulous adventurers', and more scurrilously went on to enquire, 'whether Colonel Olcott's title was earned in the war of Secession or at the bar of a drinking saloon'. Totally overwhelmed by the atmosphere of India, Blavatsky and the Colonel chose to ignore these comments and devoted their energies to travelling. In Bhurtpore in Rajputana, failing to find the Maharajah, they visited the ancient palace instead. The Colonel became quite lyrical in his account of the place:

No less than one hundred grand peacocks were strutting about on the day of our visit, swift parrots darted in emerald flashes through the air, striped squirrels flitted from tree to tree, and flocks of doves softly called to each other...[30]

They took all this as a sign that the Masters were pleased with their progress and that much knowledge would soon be revealed to them. At Agra they were spellbound by the sight of the marbled Taj Mahal, and the Colonel took to 'going native'. He dressed like a Brahmin, and wore sandals, but Blavatsky preferred to retain her decorum in Western attire.

Much occupied her mind rather than the correct outfit to wear. She was convinced that the psyche of India had been weakened, and that by studying their original roots, that of the *rishis*, the sages, the Indian people would regain the powers they had lost under the too powerful influence of the Raj. But these ruminations were not all that occupied Blavatsky, even here in India she was looking for pastures new.

She found them in Ceylon, as Sri Lanka was then known. At the invitation of two Buddhist High Priests, one of whom was already a member of the Theosophical Society, Blavatsky and the Colonel travelled to the island at the southernmost tip of the continent. They arrived, the first Westerners in the history of Ceylon who supported Buddhism. Such an accolade must have given them a cache beyond belief. They responded warmly to their reception, and this had the effect of increasing the fervour with which the people of Ceylon were to greet them from now on. Blavatsky and the Colonel might be forgiven if all this acclaim went to their heads. Almost by some divine jest, Blavatsky and the Colonel had encountered Buddhism in India, and it was this faith that they embraced wholeheartedly. They decided, almost cursorily, that the Buddha himself fulfilled all the qualifications they required of a faith, and so they abandoned their search for any other doctrine and converted to Buddhism. They 'took refuge' which is the ceremony that has at its heart an accepting of the five Precepts that underpin the Buddhist faith.

At Kandy they were permitted to observe the Buddha's Tooth. The Colonel's slightly mundane impressions of this most sacred relic are still of interest:

> ...the size of an alligator tooth...supported by a gold wire stem rising from a lotus flower...When not exhibited it is wrapped in pure sheet gold...and covered...with emeralds, diamonds and rubies.[31]

Blavatsky was convinced that it was the genuine article, and she explained to the obviously dubious Colonel that it was the Buddha's tooth 'when he was born a tiger'.

If the purpose of their conversion was to attract further members of the Theosophical Society, the ploy certainly succeeded. However, to the *Arya Samaj*, a strictly Hindu organisation, the significance of their conversion was altogether another matter. After the next meeting between Dayananda Sarasvati and the Colonel – Blavatsky was not present, the Swami did not address women – the Colonel reported that the inevitable split between the Society and the *Arya Samaj* had occurred. At the meeting, all was not entirely doom-laden, for the Colonel was enlightened as to the difference between the genuine power of the yogi and those effects achieved by conjuring or mechanical means. In the light of the accusations subsequently made against Blavatsky, for alleged sleight of hand and worse, the words have an ominous air.

In 1882 Blavatsky and the Colonel purchased a house with twenty-one acres of land for six hundred pounds, a modest sum even in the late nineteenth century. This property, outside Madras on the banks of the Adyar River is still the Society's headquarters in India. Here, the principles of the Adyar Theosophical Society were proposed and set down. The first of these was, 'To form a nucleus of the Universal Brotherhood of Humanity, without distinction of race, creed, sex, caste or colour.' This sentiment, the only one of many, even survived the schism between the Adyar Lodge and the American Lodge twenty years later.

As well as dressing as appearing to be a member of the priestly class, the Colonel discovered that he possessed the power of healing. So immediately successful was he with his first patient that:

> ...the news spread throughout the town and district...others came, by twos and threes first, then by dozens, and within a week my house was besieged by sick persons from dawn until late at night, all clamouring for the laying on of my hands.[31]

In a tragic irony, Blavatsky was diagnosed as suffering from Bright's disease a serious condition of the kidneys – she would have eight years left to live. The Colonel, however, was indefatigable, establishing nearly fifty new branches of the Society in India. In addition, he was often the brunt of Blavatsky's ire, whether she was railing at the world and its materialism, or the spite of the gods in afflicting her with such poor health. That she was also given to unruly tantrums, the Colonel was well aware.

In society, her fierce and independent nature did not ensure that she made friends in the Anglo-Indian community, quite the reverse. One of the reasons for this may have been her horror of alcohol, an aversion which is quite common among those who are sensitive or practise clairvoyance. Traditional manuals of magical practice greatly stress the deleterious effects of alcohol upon the initiate, and it is said that the imbibing of hashish or opium is far less harmful to the occult sensibilities. The ex-pats indulged freely in alcohol, that was the nature of things, and as a result Blavatsky felt she could not mix in their society with any ease. Her irascible temperament conspired to bring about the disapproval of others who she did encounter, and some would inevitably strive to bring about her downfall in India.

Not that Blavatsky was concerned with much that occurred upon the earthly plane at this time in her life. She was too much involved with what was going on elsewhere, namely her contacts with the Masters, Djwal Knul and Koot Hoomi. If her inner life was full of incident, then the conscious plane would soon be just as charged, for her mind was overflowing with the impressions and ideas that she had received during her sojourn with the Colonel in India, Blavatsky was eager to record her visions on paper, and more than that, she was determined to present to the world with the fruits of her speculations concerning the future of mankind. She was certain that mankind must wholeheartedly embrace a spiritual dimension in order that it should fulfil its spiritual promise. Blavatsky was about to embark on her travels once more and this time Europe was to be her destination.

6

The Secret Doctrine

...look with undazzled gaze upon the unveiled truth.
Madame Blavatsky

The burning of the Alexandrian Library, at sometime between the first century B.C. and the sixth century A.D., has always been cited as the greatest literary tragedy in history. It was supposed then that all written knowledge had perished in the conflagration. Another view, one more optimistic is that even greater repositories of knowledge always existed, hidden in other locations throughout the world. Blavatsky may have been aware of these histories or not, but she was certain that 'a very old book', the *Kiu-Ti*, was secreted in the Kara Korum Mountains in Western Tibet:

Pilgrims say that the subterranean galleries and halls under (the mountains) contain a collection of books, the number of which, according to the accounts given, is too large to find room (for) even in the British Museum.[32]

Apparently this remarkable work contained Kabbalistic references to Adam, the *Shu-King* (The Chinese Bible), and The Egyptian Sacred Volumes of Thoth-Hermes, the *Puranes* of India, the Chaldean Book of Numbers, and the Pentateuch. Blavatsky always insisted that she had once visited the 'Forbidden Land', the region that lies beyond the Himalayas, when she had been in Tibet during the period of her 'travels'. Its existence meant that the material proof of her thesis – that all knowledge was derived from one source – vindicated all that she had proposed in her previous work *Isis Unveiled*.

Blavatsky maintained that the *Kiu-Ti* was a commentary on *The Stanzas of Dzyan*, sacred writings written in 'a language unknown to philology'. She also believed that these writings originated from divine beings and from this conviction came her notion of the 'root races', the origins of human beings and the stages of their subsequent progress and development. This notion forms a large part of *The Secret Doctrine* and, in addition to becoming a mainstay of Theosophical principles has given rise to much debate, much of it critical.

The notion that ancient knowledge far surpassed our own was espoused by Blavatsky, and debated further by Maurice Maeterlinck, the symbolist writer, in 1922:

> We can hardly dispute the fact that the priests of India and Egypt, and the Magi of Persia and Chaldea, had a knowledge of chemistry, physics, astronomy and medicine...the great pyramid of Cheops...propounds a whole series of riddles...An occult tradition has always affirmed that this pyramid contained essential secrets...it is obvious that the priests sought to conceal it...and all this miraculous knowledge...was deliberately and systematically buried... Does not the revelation of such a mystery...permit us to suspect that many other mysteries of various sorts are awaiting...similar revelation...[33]

Blavatsky was not the first to attempt a synthesis of beliefs. Philo of Alexandria, the Jewish philosopher, born in 20B.C, dedicated his life to bringing about an exegesis between Greek philosophy and Judaism. 'Philo attempted to prove in the Scriptures the wisdom of all peoples...' [34] as Adolph Franck the Jewish scholar tells us, and he continues in another vein, 'The Kabbalah is the only religion from which all other cults emanated.' [35]The link between the Pentateuch and the Qabalah is undeniable, and a claim may be made for the latter's supremacy over other faiths.

If we consider Blavatsky's attitude to the Qabalah, the most significant esoteric system of the Western Tradition, it becomes clear as to the lengths she will go in order to uphold her own view. Blavatsky's instinctive reaction to the 'Tree of Life' was that it was at best incorrect, and at worst sinister, being allied to 'magic'. She later, grudgingly one suspects, included the Qabalah as an original source of wisdom, but in the same breath dismissed it as a mere copy of the ten *Prajapatis*, the 'Lords of all Being', or creator gods.

In 1885 Blavatsky began work upon the book that was to eventually become *The Secret Doctrine*. She was staying at the Chateau d'Enghien in France with her retinue. A spacious property, owned by Countess d' Adhemar, one the aristocratic sympathisers that Blavatsky had gathered about her in Paris, the location inspired her to plan the follow-up to *Isis Unveiled*. She worked on *The Secret Doctrine* intermittently from then onwards, particularly in Wurzburg, where she later took lodgings in the Ludwigstrasse. Here, yet another aristocrat, the Countess Wachtsmeister became her devoted companion. It is difficult not to conclude that countesses were thick on the ground in Victorian times, particularly around Blavatsky. A photograph of Wachtsmeister shows her in middle-age, resembling an old Teutonic goddess, a figure that would not be out of place in an opera by Wagner.

Blavatsky was cheered by having the Countess as her secretary, she wrote, the countess copied – it was an ideal arrangement. Blavatsky's work routine at this time of her life is impressive. She:

...would get up at six a.m. and work an hour or so before breakfast at eight. After breakfast, she would return to her desk and work till lunch-time. The Countess would summon her to the dining-room by ringing a little hand bell. Frequently H.P.B would go on working and ignore lunch. At seven she stopped work and spent the rest of the day playing patience. At nine she went to bed with the Russian newspapers under her arm.[36]

Thus, gradually the work began to take shape and Blavatsky was enthusiastic enough about its progress to write to A.E. Sinnett and confide in him of her researches. In her correspondence to him she reveals that 'all the Patriarchs from Adam to Noah' have shared their secrets with her. Blavatsky states that she will demonstrate that the most sacred writings known to man are far from a fiction, and truly represent a 'Universal Secret Doctrine' – a wisdom known to every initiate, and one that underpins every faith. Blavatsky announces that The Mysteries have been revealed to her, and she is privy to all knowledge. This is heady stuff, and reveals an inspired approach. She has abandoned the deliberate and intellectual method she often employed to produce *Isis Unveiled*. Perhaps the absence of the Colonel was significant, as if Blavatsky felt confident enough that she no longer felt she must refer to his opinion as to the worth or relevance of the material she produced.

Blavatsky had studied Hatha, Raja and Tantric Yoga, and as a result espoused the principles of liberation and purification of the mind and spirit intrinsic to all three disciplines. A fourth, Janna Yoga, had taught her that any conception that cannot be expressed will eventually form a mental picture – a representation of that particular idea. The wise student rejected each version as it appeared, though they could become successively more attractive, until he reached a stage of seeing when the 'absolute truth' was revealed. Yet again, this too is an illusion, but it is the 'pinnacle of truth'.

It was Blavatsky's aim to depict this elusive quality in *The Secret Doctrine*, and to make it central to her theme. Much writing upon the Qabalah attempts to achieve the same end. *Kether*, and the Three Veils above that Sephiroth in the Tree of Life, embody the same principle that Blavatsky is striving to describe. The similarity resides in a belief that the origin of the Kosmos is 'Divine Thought'. *The Secret Doctrine* continues on from *Isis Unveiled* in its attempt to account for the origins of philosophy, science, and religion. Various opinions upon such topics as symbolism, science, anthropology and even geology are included in its pages. Blavatsky continued with her effusive correspondence to A.P. Sinnett, revealing that the Masters provided her with visions that she described as, '…pictures, panoramas, scenes, antediluvian dramas…'[37]

In 1886 the spirit may have been willing but the flesh was most decidedly weak for Blavatsky. In the winter of that year she appeared to be almost near death, but she rallied, and informed the Countess that the Master had assured her she would be given the time to finish *The Secret Doctrine*. On being given this guarantee from on high, she reverted immediately to the physical plane and called for coffee and her tobacco box. The Master had also informed her that she must leave Ostende and journey to England. Duly, by May 1887 Blavatsky was ensconced in Upper Norwood, a suburb of London.

Her accommodation was 'Maycott', a small cottage house that belonged to Mabel Collins, the occult novelist. W.B. Yeats, the flamboyant Irish poet, visited Blavatsky there, describing her as, 'a sort of old Irish peasant woman with an air of humour and an audacious power.' The impression did not dissuade W.B. Yeats from later becoming a member of her Inner Sanctum, though not longer after he was 'with great politeness…asked to resign.' Blavatsky had expounded to Yeats upon 'the serpent power', and Yeats would later refer to her as 'a pythoness'.

Her venom seems to have been directed at the one person who took Blavatsky into her bosom. By the summer of 1887, Blavatsky having taken over Collins' cottage – a room had been put entirely at her disposal, her routine was unalterable, rising before 7a.m., writing all day and entertaining fellow theosophists in the evening – she began to abuse her host. Her behaviour seems unjustified, particularly as Collins was paying all her guest's expenses. As Blavatsky had been unable or unwilling to be part of the London Lodge of the Society, she convened a 'Blavatsky Lodge', consisting of twelve disciples. Blavatsky then vehemently insisted that such an inner circle, required sufficient space in which to convene. 'Maycott', she rudely informed Collins, would simply not fill the bill. Blavatsky then succeeded in persuading the Keightley brothers, two members of the circle, to put a larger house at her disposal, and with the general bustle that accompanied all her doings moved out of Maycott...

Situated at 7, Lansdowne Rd. Holland Park, the new 'Lodge' permanently housed Blavatsky, the Countess, and a pair of anonymous Theosophists, and was furnished completely at the Keightleys' expense. The two brothers were university graduates with 'an ample fortune'. Archibald Keightley, known as 'Archie' was the more exotic of the two, sporting long wavy hair and a dashing beard, while Bertram was a staid, archetypal Victorian gentleman, with neatly parted tonsure and equally precise moustache. Having no need to take conventional employment, the brothers offered their help with the research required for *The Secret Doctrine* and were only too glad to spend their time checking quotes in the British Museum.

The Secret Doctrine was, at this stage, a worse muddle than its predecessor. Eventually, with the aid of this 'inner circle' it was put into some sort of order. The editing and composition, 'with her (Blavatsky's) approval' seems to have fallen largely in the lap of the Keightleys. A.P. Sinnett's offer to be part of the composition process had been accepted, with certain restraints. Blavatsky referred to him as a 'chandelier', her quaint but not complimentary term for him as 'a source of light'. His role was limited to suggesting 'elegant English', for the text, Blavatsky describing him as being fit only for 'mechanical arrangements, literary not metaphysical'. The work continued unabated until at some point Blavatsky made this pronouncement. 'It is written in the service of humanity, and by humanity and the future generations it will be judged.' With that epigraph, she effectively resigned *The Secret Doctrine* to its fate.

The immediate task of the faithful few, those who were determined to see the work appear, was to see that the work was made presentable. The first task was to have the whole professionally typed, and this completed, it was considered wise to divide the work into two volumes. The first was to be titled, *Cosmogenesis*, the second, *Anthropogenesis*. Harsh reality then intervened when it became obvious that no publisher would take *The Secret Doctrine* on any realistic financial terms. It is as well that the Keightley brothers had become such major players in the saga. They agreed to cover the expenses involved in publishing *The Secret Doctrine*. Without their financial aid, the book might never have appeared.

With this decision to self-publish, the Theosophical Publishing Company was born. A circular was issued announcing that the publication date would be October 27th. 1888. The work boasted a 'copious index and a glossary of terms'. A detailed description of the contents of each part of the two volumes was also included. The price was two guineas, or a subscription copy could be obtained for one pound and eight shillings. During the various delays in publication, those who had already subscribed were offered a refund of their investment, but apparently no one did, it seemed they were content to wait patiently for the appearance of Blavatsky's second major work. By some divine providence, it was reviewed by one Annie Besant. As a result of encountering the work, this renowned socialist and atheist became, almost overnight, a theosophist. She also went on to become a figurehead of the Theosophical Society, and to many was considered even more renowned than its founder.

For Blavatsky writing *The Secret Doctrine* had surrounding it all the usual drama that was a part of Blavatsky's life. It has even spawned a book by Boris De Zirkoff, which details with exacting chronology *The Secret Doctrine* from conception to birth. Copious correspondence between Blavatsky and the Colonel, A.P. Sinnett, Countess Wachtsmeister and W.Q. Judge had ensued before the book was even halfway complete. Reading these communications gives a graphic picture of Blavatsky's emotional state during the writing of *The Secret Doctrine*. She had been particularly shaken halfway through her efforts by the appearance of the final report from the Society of Psychical Research.

Of this we shall deal with elsewhere, but it must be said that the wholesale condemnations of her in the report affected her deeply. Although she gave the impression of being impervious to criticism, this was not actually true, and, more than ever, she felt betrayed and vilified by the world. The ordinary stresses that accompany writing a book, combined with her failing health, and the onset of a debilitating melancholy, all contributed to making *The Secret Doctrine* a burdensome task. It is a tribute to her courage and tenacity that it was not abandoned at any stage.

Blavatsky would need even more fortitude to withstand the criticism that inevitably greeted the publication of *The Secret Doctrine*, most of it with the same tone as that which greeted *Isis Unveiled*. She was, however, mercifully spared the 'literary' controversy that her works began to arouse a few years after her death. This is an unedifying tale, and does little to enhance Blavatsky's reputation, precarious as it always had been. The seeds of suggestion that much of Blavatsky's material was plagiarised had been sown at the time when her works were published, and eventually this bore poisoned fruit.

An essay of 1893 by William Emmett Colman and included in *A Modern Priestess of Isis*, the less-than-flattering account of Blavatsky by Vsevold Solovyoff, set out to provide proof of this practice. Colman cites some two thousand passages of text that he believed were copied into *Isis Unveiled*. So much for the transcendental help of the Masters! Colman suggests that these additions were introduced in such a random manner as to imply that Blavatsky did not even understand the meaning of them. Colman's unflattering conclusion is that, not only did Blavatsky steal ideas willy-nilly from over two hundred books; the very words she copied were mostly alien to her. Colman, by means of an equally thorough analysis of *The Secret Doctrine* believed Blavatsky was also guilty of plagiarism when she wrote this work. He is also dismissive of the Koot Hoomi letters to Hume and Sinnett, describing them as, '...contain(ing) garbled and spurious quotations from Buddhist sacred books, manufactured by the writer to embody her own peculiar ideas...'[38]

Perhaps even more damning is the suggestion, from other parties, that Blavatsky cribbed much of the content, and perhaps the basic themes of both *Isis Unveiled* and *The Secret Doctrine*. It is said that her sources came from a little-known work by Godfrey Higgins, an author and archaeologist mostly active in the eighteenth century. *Anacalypsis* was a two-volume work published between 1833 and 1836 in a limited edition of only two hundred copies. The work is rare, and although it has been reprinted three times since its original issue, still remains so. Some years previously, in 1829, Higgins announced he was preparing a work which would prove that:

'all the ancient Mythologies of the world, which, however varied, and corrupted in recent times, were originally ONE, and that ONE founded on principles sublime, beautiful, and true.'[39]

The *Anacalypsis* duly appeared the result of twenty years of research to discover, 'a most ancient and universal religion from which all later creeds and doctrines sprang.' [40] Higgins believed that a secret religious order, which he named *Pandeism*, had once extended its influence all over the world, and that a universal principle was at the foundation of all creeds. This all sounds remarkably similar to the core of Blavatsky's two major works, and indeed to the *raison d'etre* of the Theosophical Society itself. The structure of both *Isis Unveiled* and *The Secret Doctrine* bears an uncanny resemblance to *Anacalypsis*, the only difference being that the occult element is absent. Blavatsky seeking to distance herself from this may now be seen as not a matter of principle but a deliberate editorial policy. Even more striking is Higgins' definition of what he actually names, 'the secret doctrine'. It is essential to quote his own words:

> ...What is the secret doctrine? The mythos, the parable, is the fable under which the mystery is concealed; the mystery is the secret doctrine taught by Pythagoras, by Jesus, by Mohamed – the renewal of cycles, the inspiration with the holy ghost of persons, in every cycle, to teach mankind the doctrine of a future existence of happiness or misery, according to their conduct in life.[40]

Here we have it – the acknowledgement of karma and reincarnation as being the axis around which all religion initially revolved, and its preservation in the Eastern tradition. Higgins studied Law at Cambridge, and being an academic of some standing, presents a thesis which is more closely argued and more comprehensive than Blavatsky's, but it is essentially the same. Blavatsky was inclined to present her arguments with such overwhelming passion that it was always difficult, and dangerous, for anyone to suggest that there might be another view. It would seem that her major works, the writing on which her reputation rests, might be termed 'Higgins with attitude'.

Plagiarism has always been regarded with horror in the academic world, although it has never been entirely eliminated, the temptation to take short cuts and avoid time-consuming, tedious research being too great for some students and even tutors. The issue has become more acute of late, with the very real possibility of students copying information *verbatim* from internet sites, or actually commissioning a tailor-made essay. If Blavatsky was guilty of the wholesale theft of her themes and ideas, we are left with a situation where our trust in her will be severely tested.

It has always been suggested, and with some good reason, that Blavatsky planned two further volumes of *The Secret Doctrine*. The non-appearance, or even disappearance, of these works has given rise to all sorts of fantastic legends. If Volume III and IV really did exist, it is most likely they were a composite of left-over material from the original work. Blavatsky is supposed to have discussed the content of these two succeeding volumes, saying that her intention was to provide practical teaching that would further the theories of Volumes I and II. She described a further exploration of, in a rather florid phrase, the 'impenetrable jungle of the virgin forests of the Land of the Occult'. A slightly sinister suggestion that Annie Besant suppressed or actually destroyed these two missing volumes has always been rife. The theory is that her own teachings were so opposed to Blavatsky's that she wished to expunge all memory of her from the Theosophical Society.

For Blavatsky, there was to be little writing after *The Secret Doctrine*, but inevitability what there was perhaps inevitability produced antagonisms. On May 25th. 1887 the Blavatsky Lodge – the 'Inner Sanctum', met for its second meeting, and it was then decided to produce a magazine. The Colonel had declined to publish some of Blavatsky's later submissions to the main theosophical magazine, *The Theosophist*, so Blavatsky was looking for a new outlet for her views. It must be assumed that relations between her and the Colonel had somewhat cooled, though in 1888 the Blavatsky's Lodge had been proclaimed by the Colonel as 'The Esoteric Section' of the Theosophical Society.

With his continued residence at Atyar, the business of the Theosophical Society in that continent was effectively under his aegis. The Colonel had been left in India, and Blavatsky would see neither one again.

Despite opposition by some members of the group it was decided to name this new publication *Lucifer*, Blavatsky vehemently asserting that the meaning of the word – 'light bringer' – was more than appropriate. The newly-formed Theosophical Publishing Company would produce the new magazine. Naturally, Blavatsky would be the editor and Mabel Collins – her former 'landlady' – the co-editor. It was this secondary appointment that would cause friction, and to gain some knowledge of the reasons for the further deterioration in their relationship, we must look at the character of her editorial colleague in some detail.

Mabel Collins, although not considered to be a major figure in the Theosophical world, was intimately associated with Blavatsky from the time that she arrived in London, until her death. She was twenty years younger than Blavatsky and in her lifetime Collins wrote forty-six books, a considerable achievement from any standpoint. She is most celebrated for *Light on the Path*, a series of altruisms much in line with Blavatsky's *dicta* for a pure spiritual existence. The section on *Karma* is particularly impressive, and implies that Collins, although embracing Theosophical principles, had a familiarity with the esoteric knowledge at the heart of the Western Magical Tradition.

Probably her most well-known novel is *The Idyll of the White Lotus*, published in 1885. A dream-like tale of a youth who becomes a magus and is later drawn into a web of conspiracy in the temple where he resides is, one assumes, a reflection of Collins' predilections. A goddess figure is the 'Lotus Lady' of the title, and there is much play with imagery that includes the mother, childhood and innocence. The garden in the story appears to be a symbol of freedom, and purple passages abound, much in the manner of Oscar Wilde or Ronald Firbank. Ostensibly set in an exotic East, it is but a pasteboard world that is being described. The theme is the time-honoured struggle between good and evil, but the characters are so insubstantial that they meld into each other, and more murky shadow than light and shade.

Based upon the evidence of her sister-in-law, Collins is supposed to have written the prologue and the first seven chapters of the novel with her eyes closed. Guidance from the higher planes was cited for this unique method of composition, and there is an obvious parallel with Blavatsky's methods. Did this mutual gift for clairvoyance draw these two personalities together? Collins was already renowned as a medium, but in her own case, no Masters were involved. To her, divine inspiration was personified as a procession of white-robed priests who, one day entered her house, and ascended the stairs to her room. From 1878 onwards this phenomenon had occurred regularly. By 1893, after she had acquired and refined the technique of altering her own consciousness, she constantly had 'out of body experiences'.

The enigmatic dedication of the book, 'To The True Author, The Inspirer of this Work, it is Dedicated' brought its own calumny. Perhaps in a bid to curry favour with Blavatsky, Collins seems to have confessed that Koot Homi was the true author of the work. Not receiving a good response from Madame, she thereafter denied making the claim. An irony, that the day upon which Blavatsky died was henceforth known as 'White Lotus' day, is only another bizarre aspect of the whole affair.

Collins, even away from authorship and the Society, had an eventful life, and among these extraordinary happenings was her relationship, with a man who is high on the list of suspects as 'Jack the Ripper'. In 1891, fascinated by an article in the Pall Mall Gazette on magic, Collins wrote to the author, and later arranged a meeting with him. Born in 1841, Dr Roslyn D' Onston Stephenson, as he named himself, was a self-styled magician. He was also addicted to drink and a variety of drugs. That he suffered from extreme delusions seems self-evident, and when Collins first encountered him he was in hospital with mental problems. His initial association with Jack the Ripper came when he made allegations to the police concerning the doctor who was treating him in the ward. Stephenson's actions merely cast suspicion upon him being Jack the Ripper.

Stephenson's 'magical career' was apparently inspired by the nineteenth-century writer Bulwer Lytton, whose occult novel *Zanoni* had a profound effect upon this would-be occultist. Collins became involved with Stephenson, even living with him for a time. She also attempted to establish a business with Stephenson and a friend, Vittoria Cremers, as a third partner. This venture inevitably floundered as inevitably did the relationship, particularly when Stephenson presented Collins with 'conclusive' evidence that he was actually Jack the Ripper. Whether this was a morbid fantasy on Stephenson's part is a matter for conjecture, but the result was the decline of Collins' health, both mental and physical, from that time onwards.

Before we examine the relationship between Collins and Blavatsky, we must note an association between the latter's writings and the aforementioned Bulwer Lytton. This is twofold, firstly that Blavatsky was heavily influenced by *Zanoni*, and that a subsequent work published in 1871, *The Coming Race*, has as its theme a race of initiated supermen – masters of nature who possess powers of telepathy and telekinesis. Bulwer Lytton has often been dismissed as a sub-Dickens figure whose prose is ridiculously florid, though some regard him as a genuine occultist. Bolstering the latter view is that Lytton was an active member of the Rosicrucian Society, and had a perceptive under-standing of astrology. More significantly to the occult fraternity, his description of the 'Guardian of the Threshold' is considered to be proof that he could have only encountered such a figure in the astral realm. This entity, sometimes referred to as the 'Watcher on the Threshold', is regarded as either the accumulated evil of the zeitgeist, or the negative thoughts collected by an individual during their lifetime.

In a bizarre postscript to the Stephenson episode, Blavatsky herself attributed as her own work an article he had written in 1890 on African magic, entitled Tau–Triadecta. Stephenson too claimed to have travelled in Europe, Asia, Africa and India, much as Blavatsky claimed to have done so in the earlier part of her life. Both parties were captivating storytellers, embellishing their own part in some historical incident such as fighting with Garibaldi, an incident common to tales told by them both, and both indulged in drugs. The link between these personalities can only be described as extraordinary, and explained perhaps only by resorting to that catch-all solution – past lives.

Whatever the arcane reasoning behind the quarrel between Blavatsky and Collins, the incidents surrounding The Blossom and the Fruit – a piece by Collins serialised in Lucifer – certainly provide some insights into Blavatsky's state of mind at this time. The tale, later published as a novel, has the sub-title 'The True Story of a Black Magician'. One senses that from the beginning Blavatsky was uneasy about its inclusion in Lucifer. The extent of her feelings were dramatically demonstrated when she decided to write the final chapters of the tale herself. Blavatsky wrote that "Collins lost control of the story", which might be interpreted as an editorial decision about its literary merits – the real reason is very different. Blavatsky's 'intervention' as she described it, might have been prompted by the story endorsing black magic, a view the editor could not condone, but other motives seem more likely.

Vittoria Cremers, close friend of Collins, was informed by Blavatsky that she knew Collins and Archie Keightley had practised black magic and tantric worship together. As a result,

Blavatsky maintained that she had to rescue them from demonic influences. Cremers was incredulous, even more so when Blavatsky then asked her if she would take over the financial running of the magazine. Cremers agreed and moved into the house at Lansdowne Rd. Whether she anticipated Blavatsky's next move is uncertain. On February 15th. Collins' name was removed from the magazine. Neither was Collins permitted to be part of the new community. Blavatsky accused her of 'treachery and disloyalty' and summarily dismissed her from the Esoteric Lodge. Their relationship had now soured to the point that Collins took legal action for libel against her. It may seem extra-ordinary to us how speedily individuals resorted to the law in these times, and how often such cases actually went to court. That said, Collins' case was unsuccessful, and the stress took its toll on her health – she suffered a nervous breakdown.

As to why Blavatsky behaved so viciously, one can only surmise that Blavatsky was jealous of Collins, and with good reason. She was twenty years younger than Blavatsky, attractive and sexually experienced. She was provocative and liked to flirt, and these attributes Blavatsky most definitely lacked. She takes a side-swipe at Collins' worthiness as a marriage partner by revising one of her stories to have a character say cynically:

'...there is no such reason why he should not marry, if he likes to take risks of that lottery where there so many more blanks than prizes.'[41]

Whether she admitted it or not, Blavatsky enjoyed her power and others felt they must always defer to her. Collins was someone close to Blavatsky who also had power over others, but in a more subtle way. Blavatsky could never compete with her in the Courts of Love, thus she chose to be censorious, puritanical and ultimately bitter.

Blavatsky would brook no rivalry. Vittoria Cremers would

take over the publishing of *Lucifer*, and with the arrival of Annie Besant, who Blavatsky had decided would be her successor, she simply preferred not to have Collins around. It can be speculated that Blavatsky also saw Collins as an 'astral rival'. Blavatsky was mistaken, Collins' esoteric interests were wider than her own, and centred on different concerns. The episode does not show Blavatsky in a good light. It was understandable that the 'old lady', as she was now referred, had fixed views about what was good for the Society. Blavatsky makes a thinly veiled reference to Collins practising black magic in *The Key to Theosophy*[42], and suggests that dire karmic consequences will follow her 'slanders and lies'. The same book also contains the following stricture to members of the Society, and one might see in it a not so veiled relevance to Madame:

'Never (to) back bite or slander another person. Always to say openly and direct to his face anything you have against him. Never to make yourself the echo of anything you may hear against another, nor harbour revenge against those who happen to injure you.'[43]

Anthony Powell the English novelist, once made the telling remark, '*In Vino Veritas* possibly, *In Scribendum Veritas* definitely.' That a writer reveals their state of mind when pen is put to paper seems inarguable. Blavatsky was well aware her end was in sight, and felt no need to conceal her thoughts or her feelings. As Dr. Johnson so famously remarked, 'The prospect of being hanged in a fortnight concentrates a man's mind wonderfully.' Nowhere is this more clear than when Blavatsky ostensibly turns *The Blossom and the Fruit*, Collins supposed orgy of darkness and sorcery, into a tale of light. By examining Blavatsky's text, the reader cannot help but surmise that here is a warning almost addressed to herself, combined with a confession that she too has been tempted to abuse her own powers. It is necessary to quote certain passages at length, to demonstrate just how intense were Blavatsky's emotions at this point in her life:

> You must give up for ever your love of power, and swear solemnly within yourself that you will never use the powers you possess for your own ends again. You must do this willingly. Go over in your mind the many delusions to which you have allowed yourself to succumb.[44]

Are these not the words of an initiate who has travelled far along the path, a highly-developed soul who is reviewing their spiritual achievements, knowing they have but a little time left in this incarnation? It is a tribute to Blavatsky that she could still undergo this kind of self-examination, and be prepared to scourge herself with the truth. Though the dialogue of a fictitious character, between the lines is a call from the heart. The words ring out, and no doubt she felt them echo in her soul. She is less forgiving, more accusatory, when she has the same character, in the tone of an interrogation, pose these questions, obviously aimed at Collins:

> Did you not give yourself beauty and charm in order that you might read love in his eyes ?...did you not...enchant him in order to feel the pleasure of his love for you?[45]

In a less personal aside, Blavatsky reflects with morbid resignation upon the arid souls that are all about her in the world. Her despair is the same as felt by a score of saints and sages:

> The conflicting forces on this island are terrific. It is eaten up by a giant growth of materialism springing from the blackness of its psychic nature.[46]

It is oddly fitting that in the country that was to be her final home, the one the Masters had directed her to journey to, she should find perhaps the least spiritual awareness. Yet she does not despair completely, and even touches upon the ancient heart of Albion when she continues:

> But there is a shining track right across and through the island visible to a seer; and the points on this track have always the astral flame alight. This castle is one of them.[47]

In her lifetime Blavatsky wrote a number of novels. The most interesting is *Nightmare Tales,* a collection of stories, written partly in the style of Edgar Allen Poe and often gratuitously macabre or gory. Written in the first person, at best they provide a sketch of her philosophy without the dogmatic insistence that makes so much of her 'serious' writing so leaden. The tale is set in Germany in 'a small town on the Rhine', it is confessional in style and cannot be anything but autobiographical. Most significant, is the depiction of the sage or 'Master' transmitting his teachings to his apparently sceptical pupil. Is this what Blavatsky saw in her Inner Mind when she received communications from the Mahatmas?

> At every word traced by the feeble, aged hand, I noticed a light flashing from under his pen, a bright coloured spark that became instantaneously a sound, or – what is the same thing – it seemed to do to my inner perceptions.[48]

Blavatsky's final work – *The Voice of Silence*[49] is a slim piece. The 1959 Edition contains an introduction by A. J. Hamersten takes up one third of the book, presumably to make the book of an acceptable length. Hamersten apologises on behalf of Blavatsky for her fiery and impulsive nature, but that is almost the sum total of his revelations. *The Voice of Silence* was written in Fontainebleau, a town near Paris, and it seems significant that it was the place where in the summer of 1889 Annie Besant, and a companion Herbert Burrows, would first meet Blavatsky. It is interesting to speculate as to whether it was at that moment, Blavatsky decided that Besant was to be her successor. *The Voice of Silence* is in three sections, that of the title, and two others, *The Two Paths* and *The Seven Portals*. The contents consist of Blavatsky's refinements of the *Book of the Golden Precepts*, sacred principles preserved in ideographic form upon altars in the temples of Tibet. The series, which has its own system of signs and symbols within it, appealed to Blavatsky because it was an attempt to transcend Tibetan, Sanskrit or Chinese language and present ideas in such a pure form that they could be translated into any language that the student wished. Thus, the everlasting search for a universal voice, one teaching the great truths, the Grail that sustained Blavatsky all her life, was here embodied in one artefact.

Contained in this largely idiosyncratic work are other more recognisable features such as the twelve zodiacal animals that feature in Chinese astrology, the five elements – fire, water, wood, earth and metal – that make up the Oriental system, and the seven colours that refer to the *chakras*. By making this collection of ninety aphorisms into a trinity, or triumvirate, the various parts are linked together. Of this total of ninety, Blavatsky ventured upon explicating thirty-nine, these which she claims to have learned by heart. Some are profound, others more versicles than prose, all contribute to a slight work. And these were to be the last words that would flow from the Blavatsky pen, and soon the voice would also be silenced.

7

The Masters

When there is a mystery, it is generally supposed that there must also be evil.
Lord Byron

The belief that mankind is watched over and guided by a cartel of other-worldly figures is very ancient. The, often paranoid, modern equivalent of this might be 'conspiracy theory' which is the conviction that political events are somehow engineered by secret societies in the pay of powerful governments. The earthly equivalent of the Masters perhaps began their existence in the Middle Ages. The Cathars, the Knights Templar, and later the Rosicrucians, were organisations that held clandestine meetings, and who possessed, so we are led to believe, many esoteric secrets. These organisations deliberately kept their knowledge from those in power – the monarchy and more importantly, the Church.

'High Magic' is associated with these groups – who have discovered the means to communicate with angels, and are thus party to the workings of the Divine Plan. It should be understood that 'low magic' depends, for its somewhat limited success, entirely upon the human will and the ability of that power to evoke demons. Those who persecuted the Templars and the Cathars accused them of practising various kinds of sorcery. It is no wonder that any ruling power would wish to denigrate such groups. How could any ruler feel at ease knowing that clandestine goings-on were happening beneath the very regal nose? Dissension always poses a threat to the stability of a kingdom, and only a generous leader will seek to enlighten his subjects. Most not only desire to control their behaviour, but also their thinking.

In 1795, was published *The Cloud Upon The Sanctuary* by Karl von Eckartshausen, perhaps the first study of extraterrestrial beings. That these spirits sometimes assume an earthly form seems only natural. How would man be aware of their existence if they did not do so? In the nineteenth century, the most celebrated of these were 'The Masters' – of the Theosophical Society, and the 'Secret Chiefs' – of the Golden Dawn. Of lesser known examples, Dion Fortune speaks of the 'esoteric order', and Max Heindel, as the 'Elder Brothers'. Before we examine Blavatsky's Masters, it is instructive to reflect upon the words of Samuel MacGregor Mathers, the leading light of the Golden Dawn, who had this to say of his own Secret Chiefs:

> I know not even their earthly names. I know them only by secret mottos. I have but rarely seen them in the physical body; and on such rare occasions the rendezvous was made astrally by them. They met me in the flesh at the time and place which had been astrally appointed beforehand. For my part, I believe them to be human and living upon this earth, but possessing terrible superhuman powers.[50]

In current terminology, a 'Spirit Guide', while adhering to the definition of a discarnate entity that somehow communicates with a living being, covers a wide range of identities. Thus, animals, nature spirits and angels are all included in the modern concept of a guide. Much is heard of 'Native American', 'Tibetan Monks', Archangels, and the like, and it is difficult not to feel a little scepticism when continually presented with these things *ad nauseam*. Christianity only admits one guide, Jesus Christ – the Holy Spirit, Judaism admits only Yahweh. Blavatsky's belief in the existence of the 'Masters' was the *raison d'etre* of the Theosophical Society. If the student does not accept that Blavatsky is communicating the wisdoms of The 'Masters' in her writings, they automatically lose much of their potency. These 'Masters of Wisdom', or 'Mahatmas', are the rock upon which her philosophy stands. Blavatsky concerned herself with two Masters, sometimes three. Others in the Theosophical Society, evolved systems with a greater number, and these later developments will be discussed later.

The East, particularly Tibet, did not always loom so large in Blavatsky's astral communications. Her account of meeting her 'protector' – resembling a handsome Rajput prince – has already been mentioned. In the beginning, Blavatsky's mentors were Serapis Bey, Polydorus Isurensus and John King, names which do not suggest any Oriental association. Let us examine the other-worldly credentials of this trio. Serapis Bey was an Ascended Master renowned for his stern approach, and condemnation of indulgence, adept at raising the kundalini. He was credited with constructing the temple at Luxor, and was apparently in another incarnation, Leonidas, who led the Spartans at the battle of Thermopylae. In another he was a follower of the teachings of Zoroaster and Solomon, and advised Blavatsky when she founded the Theosophical Society.

It was Serapis Bey who told Blavatsky to go to India. The identity of the last of this trio, Polydorus *Isurensus* remains a mystery. An enigma of a different kind surrounds 'John King' who seems to be a precursor, or another identity of Koot Hoomi, one of Blavatsky's later Masters. The persona of 'John King' appears to belong to a pirate of the seventeenth century, though even this is not clear, Blavatsky maintaining at one time that the name is generic for more than one spirit. At a later stage, Blavatsky was to dismiss John King as being merely the astral body of a living man, so we are none the wiser.

Blavatsky recorded encountering two of the Masters, Djwal Kool and Kuthmuni in Sikkhim, a country bordering Tibet, and spending five days in their presence. She insisted they were officials in the Lamaist Church, and this recollection was confided to A.P. Sinnett her biographer. Any more details of this significant moment, which presumably occurred during the period of travels earlier in her life, do not appear to exist. We pass on to the three more familiar 'Masters' with whom Blavatsky communicated with for a period of nearly twenty years. They were – Koot Hoomi, Djwal Khul and Sanctus Germanus. They have been assigned other names, and it was believed they had enjoyed various other incarnations.

In the Scriptures, the three Magi, or 'Wise Men', were Koot Hoomi (Kuthumi) – Balthasar, Djwal Khul (Morya) – Caspar, and Sanctus Germanus (Saint Germain) – Melchior. The previous incarnations of these Masters are numerous. Koot Hoomi was once Pharaoh Thutmose III known as the 'Son of Thoth, St.Francis of Assisi, and Shah Jahan ruler of the Mughal Empire in the seventeenth century. Master Morya was Akbar a Mogol Emperor, Abraham, Thomas a Becket, and Sir Thomas More. Saint Germain was most prolific and, among others, was incarnated as, Samuel, Plato, Joseph, Merlin, Roger Bacon, Francis Bacon and Christopher Columbus.

In aiding Blavatsky's writing, the Master Morya seems to have been of invaluable assistance. In 1885 he gave her a specific method for writing the *Secret Doctrine*. Blavatsky describes it so:

> I make what I can only describe as a sort of vacuum in the air before me like the successive pictures of a diorama, or if I need, a reference or information from some book, I fix my mind intently, and the astral counterpart of the book appears, and from it I take what I need. The more perfectly my mind is from distractions and mortifications, the more energy and intentness it possesses, the more easily I can do this...[51]

In 1904, Annie Besant appointed Rudolf Steiner as arch-warden of the Theosophical Society in Germany. In an address to the Society in 1906, he attributed the following qualities to the Masters:

Master Morya – Power.

Master Koot Hoomi – Wisdom.

Master Saint Germain – To him one applies in the case of difficulties in life.

Master Jesus – The intimate aspects of man.

The order of precedence evident in this particular hierarchy would not have appealed to Christians. It is significant, however, that the three Magi mentioned above were said to have associated with Christ during his supposed journeys in India and Tibet. According to certain authorities the Messiah also visited Persia at the same time, and it was there he met these three leaders of the Zoroastrian sect. Steiner later disassociated himself from the Theosophical Society, transferring his energies to founding the Anthroposphical Society. His conclusion after studying *Isis Unveiled* was that it espoused only an occidental view of spirituality and also that, perhaps unsurprisingly, Blavatsky was seen by him as a lunar personality. As Anthroposophy strongly embraced Christianity, Steiner was less sympathetic to *The Secret Doctrine* with its overt criticisms of Christianity.

Blavatsky maintained that the Masters lived in complete seclusion in the Himalayas. That she is prepared to identify the exact location may be that the spiritual, even exotic associations of Tibet held some weight, or she wishes to re-establish her own credentials as having travelled there. The exoteric nature of the Masters is demonstrated by their willingness to impart spiritual knowledge to anyone, provided they have the correct spiritual qualifications. The path to acquiring such wisdom is, however, beset with almost impossible tasks, making it highly unlikely, that any seeker will reach their doors.

Understanding the difference between *esoteric* and *exoteric* knowledge is essential. The former is known only to a minority, is secretive, and requires certain keys to be fully understood. It also ascertains that the divine is to be found within the individual. The latter refers to a 'knowing' independent of any personal experience – a reality accessible to all. Such 'reality' must be external, and refer to common experience, or a 'common religion'. Its followers believe in the same things, usually a divinity and the principles associated with that god. The individual philosophy related to both schools is endless, but for our purposes, let the definitions noted suffice.

The Masters came to be linked exclusively with Buddhism, which to Blavatsky and Olcott, despite their advocating a 'universal faith', was before and above all other religions. They saw in Buddhism the exoteric quality that would have had to be a major element of any world-wide faith. Buddha is regarded by the *Mahayana* school as the universal saviour and 'he who bestows deliverance', and the Master of space and time. This eternal element, and the belief that 'Buddha is everywhere in the world', may have convinced Blavatsky that the Eastern tradition was the only true path. Later Master Morya had told Blavatsky that theirs – The Masters – was the only true philosophy on Earth, and confirmed that Buddhism was the only faith she must pursue.

K. Paul Johnson, in *The Masters Revealed*, a work published in 1994, maintained that the Masters were idealisations of Blavatsky's earthly mentors. Johnson asserts that Djwal Khul was actually one Dayal Singh Majithia, a Sikh reformer. The writer tenders a list of spiritual figures, who have features in common with their aetheric counterparts. One could mention Thakar Sigh Sandhanwalia, Swami Dayananda Saraswati, Sarat Chandra Das, among several examples. The thesis is only partly sound, as few of the individuals mentioned have anything in common with each other, or indeed Blavatsky. A.P. Sinnett, who has been seen as a figure who attempted to usurp Blavatsky, making off with the Masters himself, has this to say regarding their mortal counterparts:

I had ocular proof that at least some of those who worked with us were living men, from having seen them in the flesh in India, after having seen them in the astral body in America and Europe; from having touched and talked with them. Instead of telling me that they were spirits, they told me they were as much alive as myself, and that each of them had his own peculiarities and capabilities, in short, his complete individuality.[52]

Sinnett announced the existence of the Masters in his work *The Occult World*, more importantly he portrayed them as sponsors of the Theosophical Society. In some ways, his spiritual message was bolder than that of Blavatsky by baldly asserting that the purpose of the Society was to promote certain truths that pertained to originate from a Divine Order – The Masters. It is possible that Sinnett's determination to oust Blavatsky as the only medium of the Mahatmas was founded on his conviction that the Mahatmas were one and the same as the White Lodge or Secret Brotherhood of Adepts who originated in Tibet. In this he may have been correct, but rather pettily, he refused to acknowledge Blavatsky's previously established link with this school.

Variations upon the theme being forthcoming were inevitable. Using his own idiosyncratic methods, Leadbeater was convinced he had identified a total of sixteen Masters of the Ancient Wisdom. Helena Roerich and Manly P. Hall were later to expand this concept, and Alice Bailey went as far as to suggest that there were a total of sixty Ascended Masters. All claimed to be members of The Great White Brotherhood or Lodge. Some controversy had developed over who qualified as an Ascended Master and some were even demoted to *Bodhisattva* status. The established thinking is that an Unascended Master has taken the Bodhisattva vow to remain in his earthly incarnation, in order to more fully enlighten humanity. It must be emphasised that the notion of 'Ascended Masters' as it has been interpreted by New Age pundits bears little or no resemblance to the Masters as Blavatsky conceived them.

But are the Masters, or indeed their word, to be trusted? It is a sobering experience to read this exposition, written in 1921 and prophetic of the dangerous demigods who would rise in Europe but a decade later:

> But who knows what the future has in store? When you reflect that these false Messiahs have never been anything but the more or less unconscious tools of those who conjured them up, and when one thinks more particularly of the series of attempts by the theosophists, one is forced to the conclusion that these were only trials, experiments as it were, which will be renewed in various forms until success is achieved...[53]

The question of the authenticity of the communications from the Masters was asked, and more insistently it would be asked again. The methods which the Masters chose to communicate to members of the Theosophical Society lie at the heart of any explanation. At the outset of its existence, those in the Society, besides Blavatsky, who received the Mahatma Letters were A.P. Sinnett, A.O. Hume, The Colonel, Charles Webster Leadbeater and several others. A.P. Sinnett received by far the greatest number. Although written upon paper, often in blue or red pencil, it was always maintained by Blavatsky that the medium somehow transcended its material form – the word 'precipitated' is used by her to describe the means of their creation. This involves the transferring of a mental image onto paper, and the message then being sent some physical distance. The Master's *chela* was often given the task of actually writing the astral message as it was received.

Blavatsky herself made a feature of the sending and receiving of the Mahatma letters, and in 1883 when she was established in a house at Madras, she had built the 'Occult Room'. Inside was a cupboard especially designed for the sending and receiving of communications from the Masters and called 'The Shrine'. Inside were two small portraits of the Mahatmas, and this sacred receptacle, much like an altar in a place of worship, was used only for its holy purpose. It was to be later desecrated, an act of vandalism that would have seemed unthinkable at the time it was reverently set in its place. That this act of vandalism did happen is an indication of the currents of emotion that passed between Blavatsky and those who sought to ruin her reputation.

The earliest reference to a 'Mahatma Letter' was one given to Madame Fadeef, an aunt of Blavatsky, in 1870. Apparently conveyed to her by an Oriental who 'vanished before her eyes', the main content of the letter was a reassurance that Blavatsky was in the care of the Mahatmas. As such, the reassurance that her sister was safe whilst on her travels must have been most welcome. When much energy was later expended upon attempting to demolish the worth of the Letters rather more than was been employed to defend their authenticity, the Fadeef letter was examined. Professor F.W.H. Myers of the Society for Psychical Research, assured his fellow members of the society that the letter was genuine. This relatively minor episode later became part of the investigation made by the same body. We shall deal with this episode, and its effect on Blavatsky's reputation in a later chapter. For now we shall content ourselves in knowing that in 1883 the society commissioned one Richard Hodgson to compile a report detailing Blavatsky's psychic powers. More specifically his brief was to decide upon the authenticity of the phenomena attached to the Theosophical Society.

When this report later appeared, among other serious allegations it unequivocally stated that Blavatsky had herself written the Mahatma letters. To strengthen the opinion that the letters were forgeries, Hodgson submitted them to a Mr. Sims of the British Museum, and also F.G. Netherclift, a handwriting expert.

Presumably to Hodgson's chagrin both of these experts then declared that the letters were not written by Blavatsky at all. In an extreme *volte face*, Hodgson subsequently succeeded in persuading these two gentlemen to reverse their decision! This episode is not only bizarre, but more tellingly, it demonstrates beyond doubt that Hodgson, having come to a conclusion early on in his investigations, was prepared to twist the facts to suit his own ends.

Even this threat by the Society for Psychical Research was a toothless creature compared to a sinister pair that would soon feature in Blavatsky's life. Alexis Coulomb and Emma Coulomb, the latter described as 'a weird witch-like creature, with wrinkled features', would prove to be vipers of the most vicious kind. It seems extraordinary, and perhaps a strong indication of the naivety of Blavatsky, that she would allow such people into her life.

She had first encountered them in Cairo in 1872 and they became reacquainted with her in 1879. It was a dark day when they did, and would lead to grave consequences for Blavatsky. How certain allegations made by the Coulombs, once the caretakers of the Adyar Theosophical Lodge in India, would affect the reputation of the Society in that country is discussed in greater depth later. For the purposes of this narrative it is enough to know that both stated that they had aided Blavatsky in fraudulent behaviour, including writing some of the Mahatma letters. It was a claim that was seized upon by the Society for Psychical Research and accepted wholeheartedly by them. That the Society did not investigate the genuineness, or otherwise, of any letters presented by the Coulombs, reinforces the view that the other members were prepared to accept Hodgson's findings without question.

In the present context, and to obtain a balanced view of the controversy, it is enough to quote Dr. Vernon Harrison's comments on Hodgson's document. It was purported to be an impartial and thoroughly researched appraisal of Blavatsky and the Theosophical Society. It was not. With regard to the authenticity of the letters, in 1984, Dr. Harrison examined the surviving original documents held in the British Museum as well as over a thousand colour slides. His article, on the subject, published in 1986[54] and revised in 1997, concluded that the Hodgson report was 'flawed and untrustworthy', and 'should be read with great caution, if not disregarded.'

The motive of the Coulombs, to thoroughly disgrace Blavatsky, can be traced back to their originally being dismissed for 'flagrant misconduct' by the Adyar Board of Control. In seeking revenge they first contacted Rev. George Patterson, the editor of the *Madras Christian College Magazine*, a known critic of Blavatsky. It was to him that they initially handed the 'faked' Mahatma letters. What seems equally extraordinary, in view of Hodgson's irresponsible behaviour, is that Patterson should also have so wholeheartedly accepted the word of the Coulombs. He appeared to have been convinced that the letters were faked, and immediately wrote articles in two issues of the magazine denouncing Blavatsky.

Karma, that abused and over-used word, has a bearing on the life of every one of us. Blavatsky was no exception, and if she was the product of her previous incarnations, then it was necessary that she undergo certain experiences, not always pleasant, in order to learn lessons necessary for her own spiritual progress. The law of Karma necessitates that we make amends for the actions made in previous lives. Often we are unaware of what has occurred in these lives, though sometimes hints of places we have been or people we have met are revealed to us. In the appendix assigned to Blavatsky's astrological nativity, this aspect of her character is discussed more fully. Blavatsky herself often recalled accounts of 'past-lives', and often spoke as if she was familiar with personages from the past.

For those engaged in magic or mystical activities, it is well known that the veil between the worlds is thin. For Blavatsky, it was probably almost non-existent. When Blavatsky mentioned that she 'knew' someone, she may well have been referring to the previous incarnations of that individual. That she was capable of communicating with the 'Masters' and probably with other higher beings, some who had been incarnated several times, seems beyond question. Blavatsky was often impatient with those who did not possess her understanding of things transcendental. In our own lives, there is always a possibility that we will misinterpret what others say. When dealing with a personality as formidable and focussed as Blavatsky, it seems inevitable that others would misunderstand, or mistakenly report her words.

The 'Root Races', a concept which Blavatsky detailed in *The Secret Doctrine*, received a mixed reception when it was first proposed, and has fared little better since. An attempt to codify the development of mankind and its subsequent division into various ethnic groups, it is at best fantastic, at worst racially divisive. Blavatsky maintained that a total of seven root races will eventually appear upon the Earth. At present the fifth holds sway, and the sixth will appear in the twenty-eighth century, the date of the arrival of the seventh Blavatsky did not specify.

The first root race was apparently *ethereal* and inhabited the primeval oceans. The second race Blavatsky names *Hyperborean*, and she associates with an area that includes North America, Scandinavia and Northern Asia. To this race she assigns the colour golden yellow. The third race is *Lemurian* and their land was once in the Indian Ocean, at the time when dinosaurs were on the Earth. The descendants of this race are, according to Blavatsky, the Negroid and aboriginal peoples. The fourth race is *Atlantean*, and given the speculation that surrounds the precise location of that continent, it remains unknown. Blavatsky suggested that the Mongolian, Malayan and, various other ethnic groups including Mexicans American Indians, Semites, and 'Mediterranean' peoples were the descendants of the Atlanteans.

The fifth root race is *Aryan*, which Blavatsky considered emerged from the fourth race. Their land is Shamballa, generally considered to be the Promised Land. A certain confusion as to their skin colour is apparent from Blavatsky's account. She seems to imply that other races, as they are presently known to us, will eventually become white. This fifth root race, our own, has psychic powers and has a universal purpose, such that it will establish an 'Aryan Empire' in the world. Blavatsky was less certain of the supposed characteristics of the sixth race, and we are forced to rely on Leadbeater's description of them. Not a great deal is forthcoming from his exposition except that life will revolve around an exclusively Theosophical colony in Baja, California. The seventh race, he tells us will occupy a land in the middle of what is now the Pacific Ocean, and will eventually migrate to the planet Mercury.

Quite what we are supposed to make of all this, particularly Leadbeater's contribution, is a matter for conjecture. 'The Seven Rays' is an esoteric concept dating from three thousand years ago. Gnosticism embraced the idea, as did the Catholic Church. In the East it is an intrinsic part of Hindu belief, being manifest in the seven chakras, a concept also embraced by Buddhism. In the Judaic tradition, Moses being of Chaldean descent, and thus familiar with magical precepts, would have known of the Seven Spheres, and their Seven Rays which connect to the sun.

To Blavatsky, syncretism – discovering common elements in different faiths and melding them into one universal belief – was at the heart of her mission, and became the core principle of Theosophy. Every faith having a solar principle within it, Blavatsky maintained that a corresponding feature, based upon The Seven Rays, could be found in all major religions. In *The Secret Doctrine* she cited examples of this in the mythology and beliefs of the Persian, Chinese, Egyptian and Indian schools. In her later writings Blavatsky also suggested that the 'Primeval Rays' were gods or powers, and that they had been adapted by the Christian Church as angels.

After Blavatsky, Alice Bailey is most associated with the Seven Rays. Her work, *A Treatise on the Seven Rays*, details seven emanations or eons that represent expressions of the soul-personality in an individual. Bailey's view is that the spiritual purpose of every individual corresponds to one or two of these rays. They are basically defined as follows:

1. Power and Will
2. Love-Wisdom
3. Active Intelligence
4. Harmony, Beauty and Art
5. Concrete Knowledge and Science
6. Devotion and Idealism
7. Ceremonial Order or Magic

Bailey concurs with Blavatsky's view that these seven qualities or 'impulses' make up all forms of mind and matter. According to this system, mankind is now upon the fifth ray, that of science, which seems pertinent. The world under the influence of the succeeding ray, the Sixth, would seem to be a paradise beyond the powers of the imagination.

8

Truth

There is an infinite amount of truth but it is not for us.
Franz Kafka

The motive of the biographer, and his art, is to present a rounded portrait of the subject. Key episodes in a life serve to create light and shade in the subject's character, so a thorough knowledge of these is essential. Any study of Blavatsky inevitably involves following a well-worn path. The evidence pertaining to many incidents in her life has been sifted through many times and is now as finite as it will ever be. In order to enhance our understanding of this often extraordinary character, it is necessary to attribute a motive to her behaviour whenever we may. For this, we are forced to rely on texts that are extant, trusting that they reveal as much as we would wish to know. A certain amount of speculation will inevitably find its way into any account, but this may be the lesser of two evils.

Much that has been written about Blavatsky, even by Blavatsky herself, gives a misleading impression of events. The biographer must constantly refer to the context, and when and why any account was written. If he does not he will not succeed in sustaining an accurate picture of the life. The truth is always woven from shifting, elusive material, and when the nature of the subject is equally abstruse, then the task is immense. Very quickly, what seemed at first glance to be an oasis becomes a quicksand. It is to be hoped that the features of Blavatsky have already been drawn as finely as possible, and that these concluding chapters will add the final glaze to our portrait.

Blavatsky returned to the Ukraine in the 1860s from her journeying. It was then that she began to exhibit once more those powers she had possessed as a child. Some quite startling events were documented by her sister, Mme. De Jelihowsk. One such occurred after dinner in her sister's house – Blavatsky while taking her ease in a chair, decided she wished to smoke:

> Then at the first command and look of Madame Blavatsky there came rushing to her through the air her tobacco pouch, her box of matches, her pocket handkerchief, or anything she asked, or was made to ask for.[55]

Whatever the affect upon her standing in Russian Society, Blavatsky became from that time on, a figure who was regarded with awe, if not a little fear. It was said that during her childhood the sound of bells and 'fairy music' would begin as she entered a room, and just as quickly disappear. Objects too would appear and disappear at will around her, and from this account she seemed not to have lost the talent for producing these manifestations. Blavatsky had once baldly stated that 'any man was capable of producing phenomena', and was at some pains to point out that Theosophists did not regard such happenings as miracles. She reminded her followers that the Church regarded any supernatural happenings that were not the work of angels to be, by a process of logic, the work of the Devil himself. Blavatsky also maintained that Theosophy distanced itself from such things entirely, as not being part of its ethos.

Does all this sit comfortably with Blavatsky's claims earlier in her life to be capable of performing feats which could definitely be defined as phenomenal or psychic? These included levitation, clairvoyance, telepathy, clairaudience and astral projection. She was most active in demonstrating these talents after her arrival in New York, and particularly so after meeting the Colonel. It seems at that point in her life she was determined to make a reputation for herself as an extraordinary person. Blavatsky wished to be known as someone who could cause manifestations to occur when required, and more importantly, in front of an audience. In the 1870s and 1880s, she was at the height of her powers. When challenged by the sceptical concerning her psychic abilities, she would effortlessly demonstrate them.

Magicians claim to be able to cause manifestations, and there are two methods – invoking and evoking. In the former practice, the presence of a spirit entity or guide is experienced in the unconscious – the magical imagination. During an evocation, the entity in question is seen to materialise on a conscious level. In magical terms, neither phenomenon is considered to be more significant than the other. In the nineteenth century, a spectator at a Spiritualist event would obviously be more impressed by the visual evidence of an evocation, and would have considered such things to be an essential part of the performance. Blavatsky impressed her audience by seemingly being able to produce a variety of spirits for their delectation, almost at will. Of her remarkable powers to produce objects, one example of Blavatsky's talents may suffice. While being entertained by A.O. Hume, a social reformer, who resided in Simla in India, Mrs. Hume asked Blavatsky if she could throw light on a certain problem. Her host wondered if a brooch she had given to an acquaintance, who subsequently lost the gift, could be returned. Blavatsky replied in the affirmative, and shortly after informed her host that the object was to found in the garden wrapped in two cigarette papers. A search with lanterns was made and eventually a small packet, made up of the two cigarette papers was discovered, and inside was the brooch.

The *sensorium* is the 'seat of sensation' where information about the world is interpreted by the senses. It has been concluded that the sensorium is partly created by the cultural environment of the individual.

It is significant that in the West, sight is the dominant member of the five senses, while in Russia it is touch. Perception in this culture is equated with the perceptions of the body, specifically the fingers. Does this help to explain why Blavatsky was so skilled in geomancy? It certainly offers fruitful speculation concerning her methods of manifesting objects, including the texts she needed for her writing.

The strangest talent that Blavatsky is reputed to have possessed was the power to make time pass slower. If this is correct, then Blavatsky truly was capable of 'altering consciousness', and more importantly, the consciousness of others. Awareness has its origins in the unconscious mind, the point from where all our perceptions originate, before they eventually become 'real'. It is questionable whether a finite state called 'time' exists. We are certainly capable of experiencing an absence of time – a 'timeless' state – when we experience a state of intense emotion. The immense joy that lovers experience when they are entirely absorbed in each other causes time to 'vanish'. They see only the brilliance in each others' eyes, and ordinary constraints fade away. Such intense concentration, a feeling that 'nothing else matters' creates a total experiencing of 'the moment'. An eternal 'now' exists, a state where there is no beginning and no end.

In her writings, Blavatsky mentions the *Bhikshunis* – poor, travelling Buddhists of Tibet who considered the performing of a 'miracle' – *meipo* – as being a relatively simple task. They could apparently walk in the air or upon water, regarding these phenomena as simply aspects of the divine power – *paramatman*. Their belief in *maya* – that all is illusion – made it possible for them to call upon the *Atman* – the supreme spirit – and make 'real' any visualisation they cared to imagine. The means of much that Blavatsky was capable of doing is here. She was, in shamanic terms, a 'shape-shifter'. Much of her ability is akin to the doings of Don Juan, the celebrated Mexican sorcerer whose exploits were recorded by Carlos Castaneda. Much insight into the nature of how others perceive the world can be learned from the study of this writer's works.

As Eliphas Levi was the most prominent and respected occultist of the nineteenth century, Blavatsky would have had to recognise his status concerning matters transcendental. He had too, particularly in the early stages, some influence upon her own thought. Without doubt, Levi was an enormous influence on the development of magic in the West and his writings, such as the following, powerfully written piece, would certainly have had some influence on Blavatsky's philosophy:

> Behind the veil of all the hieratic and mystical writings of ancient doctrines, behind the darkness and strange ordeals of initiations, under the seal of all scared writings, in the ruins of Nineveh or Thebes, on the crumbling stones of old temples and on the blackened visage of the Assyrian or Egyptian Sphinx, in the monstrous or marvellous painting which interpret to the faithful of India the inspired pages of the Vedas, in the cryptic emblems of our old books on alchemy, in the ceremonies practised at reception of all secret societies, there are found indications of a doctrine which is everywhere the same and everywhere carefully concealed.[56]

Very little is known of Levi, and we only glean a glimpse of his personality from his writings. Frau Gebhard was his pupil for seven years, and she describes him bluntly as a man of enormous appetites for wine and food, and little concern for personal hygiene. Levi probably considered 'tricks', the producing of marvels, to be not only pointless, but a waste of the energy bestowed by the gods upon the practitioner. The point is a simple one. For magic to succeed, power must be generated from some source, and it is not wise for the magician to behave as if he had scant regard for the origin of that power.

The popular impression of a 'magician' is usually gained from sensational films, or ill-conceived, badly written fiction. In our own times we sometimes encounter those deluded individuals who would like to own a reputation as a 'master of the black arts' or some such ridiculousness. A world of difference exists between such clods and those who actually succeed as magicians. Real magicians are dedicated to their craft, those who dabble, either fail, or become terrified when they actually experience a hint of what the whole business may be about.

Blavatsky truly owned power, and she used that force to achieve, or attempt to achieve the ends that she envisaged were best for the world. In this lies the key to solving the problem of chicanery that bedevilled her life. Her achievements were there to be seen and could not be questioned, but they were often beyond the understanding of many. Small people are satisfied only with small things, they prefer them. If they believed they had exposed Blavatsky as the perpetrator of a fraud, they were triumphant because they believed they had caused the whole edifice of her reputation to be destroyed, never again to be rebuilt. Towards the end of her life she grew impatient with those who wished to interrogate her concerning these powers. To an American-born Unitarian preacher, Moncure D. Conway, she remarked, 'It's all glamour. People think they see what they don't see; that's all there is to it.' It was a throwaway remark, but one that has unfortunately been turned against Blavatsky on many occasions and cited as a confession of fraudulence.

Concerning glamour, men were attracted to Blavatsky, but the nature of her liaisons is not easy to interpret in any meaningful manner. Her relationship with the Colonel is perhaps the most straightforward to interpret, as he was drawn into her orbit for the highest of motives. Apart from its bizarre inception, the marriage with Colonel Blavatsky is also, in some aspects, clear-cut. In contrast, the details of her next legal union, twenty-seven years later, are clouded in obscurity. Blavatsky married Michael C. Betanelly on April 3rd. 1875, and was still married to her first husband, but this did not seem to concern her overmuch. It was said that Betanelly threatened to commit suicide unless Blavatsky agreed to the marriage. No knowledge of whether this was an affectionate relationship or not, has ever come to light. All we do know is that Blavatsky divorced Betanelly three years later, on May 25th. 1878. What is more relevant is that Blavatsky became a naturalized citizen of the United States on July 8th. 1878. The question remains as to whether this was a marriage of convenience on Blavatsky's part. Did she marry an American citizen in order to pave the way towards her application for U.S. citizenship?

The most intimate aspects of Blavatsky's personal life were often discussed by those who have a taste for gossip, and speculation as to her morals was rife – rumours of her promiscuity doing the Victorian rounds. Blavatsky always maintained she was *virgo intacta* for the simple reason that it was impossible for her to have intercourse, due to *Ante flexio Uteri* – displacement of the womb. Those who wished to discredit Blavatsky by accusing her of immorality appear to have had little or no evidence for such charges, and it seems she had an indisputable reason for refuting them if she had so wished.

That Blavatsky did not consummate her first marriage seems entirely reasonable. What seventeen-year-old would wish to lose her virginity to a man three times older than herself? It is likely that such sexual encounters do occur, but are they that common? Anecdotes of sexual habits, both of excess and absence seemed to be rife in the nineteenth century, an era of repression and licence in equal measure. The occult world certainly seems to have given rise to a significant number of innuendos concerning various practitioners. Blavatsky, in her absolute lack of wishing to rely upon any man, certainly paved the way for the emergence of the 'independent woman' of the twentieth century.

Of Blavatsky's actual vices, her indulgence in tobacco did not arouse so much censure as incredulity. A woman who smoked was unusual, and Blavatsky certainly made no secret of her habit. In the Victorian era, smoking was considered an innocuous pastime, and this attitude probably continued until the 1950s, when the first rumours of a health-risk began to be whispered around in the Western world. In our own era, one that has outlawed smoking on television and in public places, it is difficult to imagine a time when heavy consumption of tobacco was commonplace. Blavatsky was certainly addicted to hand-rolled cigarettes, and so enthusiastically did she smoke, that she wore around her neck a tobacco pouch made from 'the head of some furry animal'. She also carried a large and formidable-looking knife with which she cut up raw hanks of tobacco into serviceable pieces. She would also darkly remark that she would use this weapon without hesitation upon any man who ever had the temerity to molest her.

Reports that she smoked two hundred cigarettes a day seem exaggerated; there are just not enough hours in a waking period to achieve such a feat. She rolled her own, being so deft at the practice that she could manufacture a cigarette with her left hand while writing with her right. She admitted herself that she smoked a pound weight of tobacco daily, which seems, by any standards, an extraordinary amount. The Rastafarian Reggae performer Bob Marley was reputed to have consumed the same amount of *ganja* on a daily basis. In his case, one is inclined to view this as another strand to his demi-god status as a pop star.

This reference to cannabis is not merely gratuitous – Blavatsky freely admitted to being addicted to the use of hashish at one time in her life. She had smoked opium also, but preferred the nature of the visions she encountered with hashish, believing that the stimulus to the imagination it gave was enervating in the extreme. Blavatsky was convinced that her drug experiences were as real as those she encountered on the conscious plane. She also considered that hashish gave her a profound insight into the mystery of past-lives, particularly her own previous incarnations.

It is unwise to be judgemental concerning this behaviour. The smoking of hashish, like the smoking of tobacco, was not regarded to be either as heinous or as dangerous as it might be in our more enlightened times. The medical profession is currently divided upon the issue of whether smoking cannabis results in serious mental or physical harm. The act of smoking cannot be anything but harmful, but the effects of the drug seem harder to quantify. Many stimulants, including hashish, were used as part of initiation ceremonies by the ancients so, in Blavatsky's defence, it might be said that she was following an old-established tradition. The Decadent Movement of the time, one that counted Baudelaire, Moliere and Aubrey Beardsley among its adherents, boasted of their indulgence in drugs. Blavatsky can be held to be a little hypocritical, at the end of her life, when in *The Key to Theosophy* she warns of the dangers of the use of stimulants:

> Wine and spirit drinking is only less destructive to the development of the inner powers, than the habitual use of hashish, opium, and similar drugs.[57]

The most controversial aspect of Blavatsky's life, may be summarised in one brief question – Was Blavatsky a spy? In 1877 Blavatsky decided that if she travelled to India, it would be a sensible move for her to carry an American passport rather than any Russian document. She well knew that diplomatic relationships between India and Russia were, at that time, not of the best. The Tsar had made no secret of his desire to expand his borders in the direction of the Asiatic and inevitably, Mother India was apprehensive. Russian citizens in India could easily be taken for spies and expelled from the country. When it came to the actual formalities, Blavatsky suffered no small pangs. Was she not swearing total allegiance to the United States' Constitution, and forever renouncing her loyalty to the Czar and to Mother Russia? The relationship that a Russian has with their country is potent, complex and swathed in unfathomable emotions. That Blavatsky agreed to almost abandon her native land is evidence of a pragmatic streak in her character that began to show itself more and more. She never again returned to Russia.

Six years earlier, while still residing in the Ukraine, Blavatsky had suggested to the Russian intelligence agency – the Third Section – that she might be useful to them as a secret agent. Her letter of application included the following:

During these twenty years I have become well-acquainted with all of Western Europe. I zealously followed current politics not with any goals in mind, but because of an innate passion; in order better to follow events and to divine them in advance, I always had the habit of entering into the smallest details of any affair, for which reason I strove to acquaint myself with all the leading personalities, politicians of various nations, both of the government factions and the far Left. I am writing this letter with the aim of offering my services to Your Excellency and to my native land...[58]

Her offer was not accepted, and any number of reasons may be cited for the Russian government's lack of enthusiasm to recruit her. The most likely is that they were aware of Blavatsky's association with revolutionary movements in Europe. As we will learn, an insidious suggestion that Blavatsky's reason for being in India was to encourage disaffection towards the British rule, was propagated by those who bore her ill-will. The resulting confusion as to Blavatsky's true loyalties left her in limbo. As she said herself at the time:

...I stand a spy, a beast in the eyes of England and a heartless, unpatriotic wretch in those of every Russian I honour and love, including my own sister...[59]

Blavatsky behaved in a particularly naïve manner whenever she was involved in politics on any level, be they those of the Theosophical Society or the international stage. It was a *metier* she would have been advised to leave well alone. She made a grave error if she thought that she could resolve the problem of bringing together her spiritual affinities and her natural patriotism:

> I love my country men and country dearly – but I love India and the Masters still more, and my contempt for the stupidity of the Russian Government and diplomacy knows no bounds.[60]

With her volatile temperament, particularly with regard to Mother Russia, Blavatsky was not capable of achieving such a delicate balancing act. She attempted to run with the hare and the hounds, and more besides. Her motive or methods are not the same as an opportunist – she is simply out of her depth – she is no politician. Neither would she have succeeded as spy or diplomat, because she was not even a realist. She wanted to do the best for India, and perhaps mistakenly saw the Russian interest in that country as being more beneficial to the inhabitants than the existing British rule. History has shown that she was wrong. With all her psychic powers, Blavatsky did not predict the Russian Revolution, nor did she foresee the granting of independence to India in 1947. She had informed W.B. Yeats that, 'the power of England would not outlive the century', which perhaps indicates that her clairvoyance was most apposite when she was at an emotional distance from the object of her scrutiny.

9

Friends and Enemies

The aim of those who follow this Path is to obtain complete mastery over every aspect of created life.
Dion Fortune

Blavatsky's relationship with others was often stormy. She attracted, as any public figure, 'fair weather friends', and she also encountered those who ultimately wished to harm, either her standing or her spirit. A stain upon her reputation is still evident, and it is there as the result of a concerted campaign by a few unpleasant individuals to malign her. The 'chief weasel' appeared in 1884 when Blavatsky visited France in the company of the Colonel. They landed at Marseilles, and travelled to Nice where they were to be the guests of Marie, Lady Caithness, Duchesse de Pomar, and President of the French branch of the Theosophical Society. In Paris, this extremely wealthy woman put an apartment on the Left Bank at the disposal of Blavatsky and the Colonel, and it was in these plush surroundings that Blavatsky met a journalist – Vsevold Solovyov.

He was the brother of Vladimir, the latter a respected, though somewhat dour, writer and philosopher, and the inspiration for Dostoevsky's characters Alyosha and Ivan Karamazov. Vladimir had studied Gnosticism, the Kabbalah and most remarkably, claimed to have had personal experience of Divine Wisdom in the person of Sophia. His obsession was to bring about a reconciliation between Roman Catholicism and the Russian Orthodox Church, the beginning of a plan to bring together other faiths in a syncretic system. Blavatsky and Vladamir might well have had a lot of philosophical ground in common, but unfortunately it was the less attractive Vsevold who entered her life. It is to be surmised that this rather odd character lived much in his more accomplished brother's shadow. In that half-darkness, his own reputation took on a disturbing hue, as we shall discover.

The Solovyov family was of Ukrainian-Polish extraction, so Vsevold and Blavatsky would have had some initial affinity when they met. At first, the two were impressed by each other, working together, as master and initiate. It did not take long, however, before Blavatsky realised that her pupil, who possessed a chronically neurotic temperament, was not suited for occult work. In 1885 she wrote to her sister of him, 'I like very much my friend Solovyov, but he says stupid things about our Mahatmas, this poor unbelieving Thomas...Poor man, I am sorry for him.' Her sympathy was misplaced; Solovyov envied Blavatsky's powers and, while appearing to be her supporter, continued to harbour feelings of jealousy and malice toward her. He dogged her footsteps in the last years of her life as she travelled in Italy, Switzerland and Germany. During this time Solovyov, in the company of six others, saw Blavatsky perform a clairvoyant feat which, at the time, he described as genuine. This involved Blavatsky copying the contents of an unopened letter onto a second sheet and adding various features to the original. He also encountered the Master Morya, in substantial form. Thus at that time Solovyov was the greatest advocate of Blavatsky's powers, and the Theosophical Society.

Suddenly, the moment when he performed a total *volte face* and became an equally strident supporter of the Society for Psychical Research, was nigh. As we shall discover this was the organisation that, with ruthless intent, endeavoured to bring about Blavatsky's downfall. Initially, Solovyov, as a result of witnessing paranormal events, appeared to lose his innate cynicism, but later regained it tenfold, and denied that the phenomena he had witnessed were ever genuine. He played a strange waiting game with Blavatsky, convinced there would be a moment when she would be so indiscreet as to reveal all her secrets to him. Solovyov, like many others, had no faith in Blavatsky's powers. He convinced himself that she would eventually confess to him that all was fraudulent, then that would be the moment he would denounce her to the world. When this did not happen, Solovyov was forced to fictionalise the events he had seen. In order to thoroughly damn Blavatsky, he ascribes these words to her as a 'confession':

'What is one to do when, in order to rule men, you must deceive them, when, in order to catch them, make them pursue whatever it may be, it is necessary to promise and show them toys?...But long, long ago I understood these dear people whose stupidity gives me enormous satisfaction...If you only knew what lions and eagles in all the countries of the world have turned themselves into asses at my whistling...' [61]

Even as a supposed paraphrasing of Blavatsky's words, the style is artificial, the tone unconvincing. Yet, along with other equally questionable evidence, and many blatant lies, Blavatsky was condemned by every succeeding generation as a cynical charlatan.

When an initiate starts upon the path every trait in his personality comes to the surface. What emerged in Solovyov's case was a bitter, vengeful character, one who believed he had been spurned by his teacher. How this sneak managed to gain the confidence of Blavatsky's sister Vera seems quite inexplicable. But succeed in this he did, and many an indiscretion came his way, some being included in the vicious little volume that he was ultimately to publish. Initially appearing in 1892 as eight articles in *Russian Messenger*, the next year it was published as a book in St. Petersburg. In 1895 an English translation appeared, *A Modern Priestess of Isis*, 'abridged and translated on behalf of the Society of Psychical Research'. As will be made clear, this unsavoury organisation had a vested interest in aiding and abetting any document that vilified Blavatsky. Even though Blavatsky's death had occurred four years earlier, there were still those who wished to ensure that her reputation would never recover, her critics gathered for an all out assault.

Solovyov was writing for a Russian public hungry for sensation, but if they believed this was going to be a lurid expose of Blavatsky, they would be disappointed. The book is a rambling, disjointed account of Solovyov's relationship with Madame, mainly in the form of letters, and recollections of conversations all from a decade before. The appendices include an abstract of a piece by Mme. Zhelihovsky, Blavatsky's sister, and perhaps most damning, an analysis of Blavatsky's writings by William Emmette Coleman. We shall examine Coleman's views in due course. Only one piece of Solovyov's text is really of any interest. This is the unflattering, but admittedly comical, description of Blavatsky's entourage while she was travelling in Bavaria. Accompanying her was Babajee, a bald Indian midget with huge eyes, and a skeletal figure, and Mary Flynn, who is described as being stout with an 'ugly red face'. Blavatsky herself was said to own a 'globular figure', and be wearing a hat like a 'fireman's helmet'.

As an ironic coda to the tale of 'fifth columnists', Blavatsky always maintained that Solovyov constantly tried to persuade her to take up this calling, he always insisting that he had enough influence with the Russian government himself to recruit her as a spy. Solovyov denied this view, and maintained that Blavatsky kept soliciting him for an opportunity to take up the role of a spy. In a further attempt to blacken her character, Solovyov announced that Blavatsky had been an agent of Okhrana, the Czarist secret service. He conveniently did not mention that he himself was working for the Parisian branch of the same organisation at the time.

Blavatsky's dealings with Solovyov are yet another example of the bizarre episodes that appear without rhyme or reason in

Blavatsky's life. If nothing else, this particular relationship demonstrates that Blavatsky's sense of loyalty was often misplaced. She had no illusions about Solovyov's character, yet still she embraced him as a friend, ignoring his so obvious defects, and even denying that they existed. That 'Master would have nothing more to do with him, all my prayers not withstanding' seems a dismissal by the higher realms, yet not enough of a condemnation for Blavatsky.

Even when she writes to A.P. Sinnett in 1886 'Solovyov has turned against me like a mad dog', her words are uttered more in surprise than anger. On this and other evidence, it is sometimes easy to see why Blavatsky's friends loved her, almost in spite of her nature. She was fickle in her affections, praising one moment and damning the next. Given that she was almost childlike in her attitudes to others, does this imply that Blavatsky was incapable of any intrigue? If it does then we have substantial proof that she was not guilty of the deviousness and fraudulence of which she was often accused. It seems certain that if she loved, she demonstrated her affection, if she did not, then she also made no secret of her feelings. Such an approach makes for deep-seated enemies as well as faithful friends. We might conclude that this black and white view of those she encountered accounts for the virulence of Blavatsky's critics.

Nearly halfway through the twentieth century, and many years after these events, one Beatrice Hastings enters the picture. A friend of George Bernard Shaw and G. K. Chesterton, while also briefly a member of the Theosophical Society in 1904, she was a devotee of the occult and particular Blavatsky's teachings. In 1936, being outraged when reading a book by Harold and William Loftus Hare that ascribed the authorship of the Mahatma letters solely to Blavatsky, she wrote a damning account of their work. Fired by the event, this tireless woman formed, two years later, as society named 'The Friends of Madame Blavatsky'. This was a public organisation intended to vindicate Blavatsky's still questionable reputation.

Hastings' main aim was to expose what she termed 'one of the most atrocious conspiracies of modern times', namely *A Modern Priestess of Isis*. Hastings was convinced that the Society for Psychical Research deceived the public by sponsoring and publishing *A Modern Priestess of Isis*. She was certain that the Society had been in possession of contemporary documents that disproved Solovyov's claims, whilst still going ahead and publishing the accusations against Blavatsky. To substantiate her claim, Hastings' also castigated a review of *Modern Priestess of Isis* by F. Podmore, a leading member of the Society for Psychical Research. It is difficult not to concur with Hastings' views, and conclude that the members of the Society for Psychical Research were trying to save face when their report was later severely criticised. They clutched at any straws to substantiate their claims concerning Blavatsky. Solovyov's inventions suited their campaign well enough, and it is why they endorsed them. We have set the scene earlier; now let us examine this singular organisation and its scurrilous attitude towards Blavatsky.

The Society for Psychical Research was founded in 1882 by Henry Sidgwick. The membership largely consisted of ex-Cambridge University men. One of the company was Frederic Myers, a member of the Theosophical Society until 1886, and a close friend of Alfred Sinnett. Originally, the *raison d'etre* of The Society for Psychical Research was to sift the mass of information that referred to the sightings of ghosts, and to decide what, if anything among this data was believable. From these modest beginnings The Society for Psychical Research became a formidable body, almost the arbiter of what was 'genuine' and what was not in the spiritual world. Initially, Blavatsky, as so often in her life took a benign view of the Society, and considered that it could be used as a platform to promote the views of Theosophy. This was not to be, and far from being benign in their attitude to Blavatsky, they were later to prove to be a thorn in her side – a sharp, poisoned barb, that injured her deeply.

The first report from the Society of Psychical Research was due to appear in the autumn of 1884. All might have been well if certain communications from India had not fallen into the hands of those who managed the Society. This information originated from the waspish, and increasingly indiscreet Madame Coulomb, the caretaker of the Society's headquarters at Adyar. Her first announcement was to reveal, to anyone who would listen, that Blavatsky owed her a sum of money, loaned to her twelve years previously and never returned. Mme. Coulomb followed this assault with making a pair of statements the first of which, considering the delicate political situation in India, might well have put members of the Society in considerable danger. This was that the Theosophical Society was set up to overthrow British rule in India. Although ridiculous, if any such idea had been taken seriously by the authorities, it would certainly have not gone down well. By 1884 the Society was finding itself with an increasingly ambivalent reputation in India, and it was not viewed kindly.

Mme. Coulomb's second accusation was much more serious, in that it struck at the heart of Blavatsky, and the Society's standing. Mme. Coulomb implied she had proof that the phenomena Blavatsky had produced for audiences in India were physically engineered, and relied entirely on a system of trapdoors and concealed cabinets. These false entrances and the like, Mme. Coulomb made clear, were all connected to Blavatsky's boudoir. From here, she claimed, it was possible for Blavatsky to engineer all manner of fakery. She added, for good measure, that the keys to this sacred chamber were now in the exclusive possession of Mme.Coulomb herself. Listening to all this, other members of the Society, among them stalwarts Damodar and Lane-Fox, sought to act quickly. They were also on the Board of Control of the Society, and responsible for Adyar, so they had the authority to remove Mme. Coulomb from her post.

They were comprehensively check-mated when they attempted to implement this move. A divine message from no less a personage than Koot Hoomi. A communication was relayed to them, it is not clear whether by astral or electronic means, but it was certainly unambiguous in its tone. Mme. Coulomb's spiritual virtues alone should reassure any critics of her behaviour that she was guilty of no misdemeanour and should remain in her position. The situation could not possibly continue for too long without there eventually being some *denouement*, and, as would be expected, it came suddenly and dramatically. Mme. Coulomb had threatened to reveal to the Protestant Missionaries the contents of forty letters in her possession, communications which she believed damned Blavatsky even more. Mme.Coulomb had gone too far this time, and she and her husband were summarily ejected from Adyar. The end was unseemly, involving scuffles and the police. It was an indication that the wolves were surrounding Blavatsky and closing in for the kill.

The First Report of the Society for Psychical Research was only issued privately. Their representative, Richard Hodgson, who had been commissioned to go to India and investigate the case, had not yet submitted his own findings. Shortly before his departure there had been a report that the text of twenty-four lines of an 'astral message' from Koot Hoomi had been plagiarised by Blavatsky from another source. Henry Kiddle, an American lecturer on Spiritualism had recognised Blavatsky's channelling as part of the content of a speech he had given and had complained to the spiritualist press. Gleefully it seems, they had reported her supposed misdemeanour. This only added fuel to the fires that were being stoked around the, as some saw it, increasingly heretical Blavatsky. The report of the Society for Psychical Research, even in its incomplete version, would now contain the damning sentiment '...it is certain that fraud had been practised by persons connected with the Theosophical

Society.' When these words were reported to Blavatsky, in her bed and extremely ill, those around her thought she was about to die.

Worse was to come. Hodgson arrived in Madras in December 1884, and remained there for three months. He came at a time when morale was low in the Adyar camp. The Colonel was not at his best, defensive and apprehensive about the accusations, fearful of the missionaries, and not resolute enough in his manner to deal with the Coulombs. Hodgson asked permission to see the 'Occult Room' which contained 'The Shrine'. After some prevarication, he and 'a party of Theosophists' entered the room, whereupon Hodgson thoroughly examined every aspect of its construction and alteration. To those who wished to denounce Blavatsky as a fraud, his findings were an indictment conclusive enough to condemn her, in the eyes of many, forever. One rather significant occurrence was missing from the report; Franz Hartmann had discovered Alexis Coulomb in the process of constructing the very passage, trapdoors and sliding panels that were at the heart of Hodgson's conclusions concerning Blavatsky. The denouncement of fakery was the result of deliberate fakery itself.

On 31st. December. 1885, the Society for Psychical Research presented its final report. It was a bloated document of 100,000 words, but the 'Conclusions of the Committee' which begins the document, were brief and as condemnatory as they could possibly be. Madame Blavatsky was 'one of the most accomplished, and interesting impostors of history'. It is a phrase that has been repeated a hundred, if not a thousand times, and has probably done more harm to Blavatsky's reputation than anything else ever written about her. The Committee's remarks about the Colonel, not 'imputing wilful deception to that gentleman', and dismissing him as 'merely a gullible fool', were equally damaging. The Committee's willingness to uncritically accept Hodgson's findings, without even examining them, is astonishing. As Dr. Harrison remarks:

Madame Blavatsky was the most important occultist ever to appear before the Society for Psychical Research for investigation; and never was opportunity so wasted.[62]

As would be expected, reactions to the report were mixed. The first contemporary defence of Blavatsky came from Alvin Boyd Kuhn. An American scholar, who was the first P.h.D student to write a doctorate upon Theosophy, he had to this to say of Hodgson:

He rendered an *ex parte* judgement in that he acted as judge, accuser and jury and gave no hearing to the defence. He ignored a mass of testimony of the witnesses to the phenomena, and accepted the words of the Coulombs, whose conduct had already put them under suspicion.[63]

Dr. Vernon Harrison, who we have already mentioned as a staunch defender of Blavatsky in connection with the Mahatma letters, published his views upon the Hodgson report in 1986, almost exactly one hundred years after the event. In support of Kuhn's remarks he wrote:

...whereas Hodgson was prepared to use any evidence, however trivial or questionable, to implicate HPB, he ignored all evidence that could be used in her favour. His report is riddled with slanted statements, conjectures advanced as fact or probable fact, uncorroborated testimony of unnamed witnesses, selection of evidence, and downright falsity.[64]

The reactions of the London Press to the report are of some interest. Most of the newspapers were contemptuous of the whole proceedings, believing the matter to be beneath their dignity, but *The Sporting Times* was robustly damning, suggesting that 'spiritualists should be sent as vagabonds to the treadmill'.

The backlash had begun earlier when the eminent Victorian scientist, John Tyndall, convinced that science had a monopoly on knowledge, castigated willy-nilly all faith of any stamp. 'The world will have a religion of some kind, even though it should fly for it to the intellectual whoredom of Spiritualism.' [65] As to Blavatsky herself, she always maintained that she would, in time, be vindicated, and in some measure she has, but it is has taken a considerable amount of years. The most nauseating aspect of the whole sorry affair is the attitude of the Society for Psychical Research, who even in 1982 was totally unrepentant. In their centenary volume[65] they still referred to Blavatsky as performing 'quasi-psychical phenomena' and referred to Hodgson as one of the 'Society's most-respected researchers'. It was a harsh fate that conspired to make a dullard, in Hodgson, and a neurotic, in Solovyov, cause untold harm physically and mentally to Blavatsky.

She had returned to India at the end of 1884 to great acclaim. Blavatsky had every intention of reclaiming her reputation in that country, but being advised not to recourse to the law, she did not take legal proceedings against the Coulombs. It was later said that she damaged her reputation even more, as her refusal to prosecute was seen as an admission of her own guilt. Having accused Blavatsky of forgery and fraud, Madame Coulomb and the Rev. George Patterson were confident that she would sue them for libel. They had heard that this was Blavatsky's intention but, to their chagrin she did no such thing. Tired of waiting, they took it upon themselves to sue General Morgan of the Theosophical camp for libel, accusing that gentleman of calling M. Coulomb a liar and a thief. The general rightly refused to apologise, and no more was heard was this increasingly malicious pair. More important, was the effect of these legal skirmishes upon Blavatsky's health. Her condition appeared so serious that the Colonel deemed it sensible for her to leave India, and this she did, never to return.

Were the sessions elaborately staged costume dramas? As the old adage insists – 'Where there's smoke – there's fire'. It is not the business of the biographer to defend a position that is indefensible, but neither is it his role to arbitrarily pass judgment. To consider this episode as part of a bigger picture, that of Blavatsky's character, is more relevant to his task. G.R.S. Mead, George Robert Stowe Mead to give him his full name, was a member of the Inner Group of the Theosophical Society and also Blavatsky's private secretary towards the end of her life. He was a respected writer on occult matters and, it is said, influenced W.B.Yeats, Ezra Pound, and even C.G.Jung.

In 1909, after twenty-five years in the Society he resigned, in protest at Annie Besant wishing to re-instate C.W. Leadbeater. He founded an occult group named the Quest Society in the same year. If anyone should have an intimate view of Blavatsky it is Mead. Of one aspect of her character, he was convinced that she was incapable of fraud, much less operating mechanical devices, or employing confederates in grandiose acts of deception. Mead knew that she was most indiscreet, in that she could never keep confidences either about herself or others. He was convinced that Blavatsky would at some time or another, inevitably confessed to Mead if she had acted with any duplicity. He had complete access to Blavatsky's papers, and asserted that if she had anything to hide she would not have given such latitude to her secretary. He described her as 'quite prodigal in her frankness', and 'incapable of fraud or concealment'.

Like many exceptional people, Blavatsky was not only enigmatic, but paradoxical. On the one hand she seemed to care not a fig for how her standing was with the world, but on the other, she appeared to care a great deal. She had the *droite de seigneur* that one associates with those born under the sign of Leo, yet often she appeared as a hunted beast licking its wounds. Blavatsky was certainly often naïve about the world and its ways, and this may have stemmed from the kind of exclusive upbringing that tends to protect those born within its confines. A tendency to behave with little consideration for the feelings of others is undeniably evident, yet her heart was always open to humanity. That she had to do battle with a material world which she saw as ignorant, hostile and unfeeling was extremely difficult. The chasm between her own perceptions and the short-comings of even her devoted pupils was enormous. Her authority to pronounce upon the ways of the spirit world she did not take lightly, she considered herself to be the voice of the highest beings it was possible to conceive. Blavatsky was nothing but sincere, and her motives always seem to be crystal clear, even when she was wrong!

She followed the principle that 'the end justifies the means', often one that is morally questionable. It was this belief, that she was somehow beyond criticism or even reproach that was often her undoing. Certain questions cannot help but be asked. Did Blavatsky seek to defend herself against her accusers, those who accused her of charlatanism and worse? If she did, what was her defence? Did she have any way of answering her critics, or did she consider it beneath her dignity to even engage with them? It is almost impossible to know the answers, for Blavatsky surrounded herself, not only with loyal followers, but with an aura of the other world. No one can take from her that absolute conviction that the 'Masters' guided her every move, that is the greatest constant in her life and it was the faith that sustained her. It is why the Theosophical Society that she founded with the Colonel, remains today as a symbol of many things, but ultimately – faith – a desire to discover the truth. The path of any spiritual seeker is the quest for the truth. Blavatsky, despite her own failings, followed that path – unswervingly, and to the end.

Of her failings, the question of her loyalty to others must come under some scrutiny. She could be utterly steadfast or ruthlessly divisive, it is as simple as that. To take one example, her relationship with the Colonel seems on the surface to be built upon rock, and the most long-lasting of any partnership she embarked upon. Yet, in 1884 she willingly agreed to participate in a *coup* to oust the Colonel from the Society. Later, when the Colonel found out, the knowledge almost drove him to suicide. Blavatsky's mental state during an illness, when the scheme was proposed, or mere pique? Either may be to blame. Sometime after, the Colonel appeared almost laconic about the incident. He is known to have once remarked with some asperity that, to Blavatsky, people were 'nothing more than pawns'. Does this concur with Solovyov's conclusion that Blavatsky's success lay in 'her extraordinary cynicism and contempt for mankind'? Let us not make our final judgement until all the evidence has been placed before us, and in some strange ways this did not occur with Blavatsky's end. Her quitting the material plane was only another step in her journey.

10

The Legacy

Wisdom alone is the right coin with which to deal, and with it everything of real worth is bought and sold. And for it Temperance, Justice, Fortitude and Prudence are a kind of preliminary purification.
Plato

Helena Petrovna Blavatsky died on May 8th. 1891. This day is known to Theosophists as *White Lotus Day.* Her body was removed to Woking, Surrey, where the only crematorium in England then in existence was located. After her cremation, the ashes were divided equally into three offerings, one each for Europe, America and India. Of the last, the river Ganges received her mortal remains. Blavatsky's final words apparently were, "Keep the link unbroken! Do not let my last incarnation be a failure!" In 1888 she had written these words to W.Q. Judge:

> ...I feel strong...ready to fight for Theosophy and the few *true* ones to my last breath. The defending forces have to be judiciously...distributed over the globe, wherever Theosophy is struggling against the powers of darkness.[68]

It is in sentiments such as these we see clearly the true face of Blavatsky, she was utterly determined that the movement she had begun should continue. Whether the Theosophical Society was as loyal to Blavatsky as she was to the organisation is a matter for debate. The impression is that those who were prominent figures in the Society were not always as altruistic as their founder. Some were merely ambitious and that is all, using the Society for their own ends. Others did not subscribe to Blavatsky's views and, when she was not there to prevent them, immediately set about altering the nature of her teachings. A coldness and an air of bloodless deliberation seeps into the Theosophical Society as soon as Blavatsky's presence is removed. It is difficult not to come to the conclusion that without its founder the Society never again achieved its former glories.

Apart from Eliphas Levi, Blavatsky was the only figure in the nineteenth century who wrote so extensively and informatively upon aetheric matters. In her work *The Secret Doctrine* the thesis was refined so that her precepts were presented as the ultimate truth concerning the higher planes. The work is much weighted towards the Eastern tradition, and it might be said that the Colonel's *Buddhist Catechism*, is a more balanced account and a key text in the understanding of Buddhism. The Colonel attempts to synthesise Eastern and Western thinking, in a way that Jung would also attempt, but Blavatsky was loath to do. Blavatsky's great strength was as a spiritual pioneer and a leader. She was the unifying influence in the Theosophical Society, and after her going the Society revolved around a sun whose light came from the energy of discord, not harmony.

Blavatsky had envisaged the Theosophical Society as a haven of study and enlightenment. In a very short time that organisation became more a political forum within the occult world than anything else. A mere eight years after the Society's inauguration, the London Lodge was in an uproar. Its officers were locked in a seemingly irreconcilable dispute over the meaning of the term 'Theosophy'. Machinations resembling intricate chess moves were afoot. A spate of resignations had even inspired a motion to be tabled at one meeting suggesting the removal of both Blavatsky and the Colonel from the Society. This failed completely, and it always seemed that while she was still alive, Blavatsky was solely in charge of the Theosophical Society.

At the centre of the dispute in the London Lodge was A.P. Sinnett, a man who as the one-time confidant of Blavatsky would find himself totally marginalised after her death. Even with Blavatsky as a mentor, he had followed his own convoluted path. He lived in a world of contradictions where spirituality and material ambition fought for precedence. Sinnett was often a disappointed man. One of the leading figures of the London Lodge, he had published *Esoteric Buddhism* and two theosophical novels, he was still not content. He had set his sights on being President of the Theosophical Society in England, and was bitterly disappointed when in 1880 Dr. Anna Kingsford was elected to the position over him.

Anna Bonus Kingsford was a remarkable woman, the first of her sex ever to become a medical doctor, she was also an anti-vivisectionist and a vegetarian. Apart from being clever and charismatic, she was also beautiful, and in any account of her she is always described so. She certainly made a strong impression on Edward Maitland, her lifetime psychic partner when they first met:

> Tall slender, and graceful in form. Fair and exquisite in complexion. Bright and sunny in expression. The hair long and golden, but the brows and lashes dark and the eyes deep set and hazel, and by turns dreamy and penetrating. The mouth rich, full and exquisitely formed. [69]

Maitland, many years her senior, enjoyed a platonic role as her psychic partner. He was probably in awe, not only of her persona, but her energy and achievements for his entire life. Kingsford was the author of *The Perfect Way*, a seminal work on Theosophy, and this had all the right qualifications for her position. Unfortunately, for the unity of the Lodge, she was a Christian mystic. Having little time for the Tibetan and Indian version, she set about defining the aims of the Society, and would not tolerate the inclusion of any 'Eastern Masters.'

Such a radical stance did not do wonders for the unity of the

Lodge, and inevitably there was a split in the ranks. This created such a ruction that Blavatsky, on receiving word as to what was going on, felt she must intervene. She hurried from Paris to London and confronted the opposing parties in the London Lodge. The Colonel's gentle hand then intervened in the dispute and a compromise was reached. The Kingsford party agreed to form a 'Hermetic Lodge' of the Theosophical Society affiliated but not attached to the main body. It was a convenient, but slightly bizarre solution, as the Hermetic Lodge had nothing whatsoever in common with the principles of the Theosophical Society. As well as 'Christian Pantheism' and the Qabalah, the Hermetic Lodge espoused the mythology of Egypt.

It is interesting that these very elements would later be the foundation of the Golden Dawn. This celebrated magical society was formed in 1888, and two of the founders Samuel MacGregor-Mathers and William Westcott often attended the lectures given at Kingsford's Hermetic Lodge.

Another prominent Golden Dawn member, Robert Felkin, was previously a devotee of the Theosophical Society. Mathers, the real force behind the Golden Dawn must have been aware, from witnessing the struggles of the Theosophical Society, of the dangers latent in any group devoted to spiritual work. It would have been fascinating to know Blavatsky's reaction to the Golden Dawn, but nothing was ever recorded. It was strongly suggested that her own Esoteric Lodge was formed in response to this new coterie.

Even with the departure of Kingsford, Sinnett's wish to lead the Society was not granted. Blavatsky had already named her successor, as we know – Annie Besant, secretary of Blavatsky's Esoteric Lodge. Apart from president, no higher rank could have been bestowed on any member, as she was responsible for disseminating Blavatsky's teachings. Besant had been bequeathed her mentor's signet ring, an object with supposedly great magnetic properties, and this alone guaranteed the role she would play in the Theosophical Society. It is a matter of some conjecture as to how Blavatsky would have reacted to Besant's subsequent introduction of new teachings into the Society's curriculum. Many regarded these as being totally opposed to Blavatsky's original doctrines.

Besant, and Leadbeater, who between 1907 and 1930 formed a close alliance, set about altering many of Blavatsky's original teachings. Leadbeater himself first ruined Blavatsky's cosmology by simplifying it. Then, by mixing it with other traditions, he made a complete nonsense of the original scheme. His crowning impudence was to claim it as his own. This new regime under Besant was referred to as Neo-Theosophy, and much opposition to these new teachings ensued. The greatest schism in the ranks of the society, was as a result of the homosexual scandal that had centred around Leadbeater. Besant was not willing to accept the charges made against her trusted colleague, so the disaffected faction took their grievances to the Colonel. A judicial committee found that there was clear evidence against Leadbeater, and this decision made it obligatory for him to resign from the Society.

The Colonel died soon after this event, and Leadbeater, having the support of Besant and the British Convention of the Society saw his membership restored. The decision scandalised the majority of the Society and prompted over seven hundred members to resign. Despite such a condemnation, Leadbeater moved to Madras where he went on to exert great influence over the Indian section of the Society, as well as being a prominent figure in the Liberal Catholic Church.

In 1894 another dispute occurred, this time between Annie Besant and William Quan Judge, one of the three original members of the theosophical Society. Like the Colonel, Judge practised as a lawyer, specialising in commercial law. In 1884 he became general secretary of the American Theosophical Society and served in that capacity for ten years. A study of his features in contemporary photographs gives the impression of an honest and trustworthy man. It is difficult to imagine that W.Q. Judge would be capable of behaving in a deceitful manner, yet Annie Besant implied that he had done so. His crime, according to his accuser, was to have forged certain letters of the Mahatmas. Besant went about publicising these accusations in a convoluted and bizarre manner, and it is difficult not to conclude that if anyone is being underhand it is her.

Articles, written by Besant, denigrating Judge, were published in various newspapers and journals. In these, Besant disingenuously states that it is not she who is his accuser. Who then? Of the letters, Besant suggests that they were communicated 'through Mr. Judge' and 'by the Master'. And what was her proof that Judge wrote these letters himself – the Master told her so! It seems that Besant was the sole arbiter when it came to deciding whether divine messages were genuine or not.

Judge, apart from questioning Besant's methods of presenting her accusations, remained stoically silent about the whole affair. He did so even until his death, only two years later. The result of all this, a schism between the American and the British Lodges, dramatically demonstrated where the loyalty of the members lay. From that point onwards, Judge presided over the Theosophical Society, and Besant and the Colonel took the title the Theosophical Society of Adyar for their Lodge. It is difficult not to regard the whole episode as an unnecessary, and unseemly, piece of political intrigue by Besant, her method of removing the old guard and setting up her new regime with Leadbeater. Even more unsavoury is that in the 1920s, during a 'private conversation', Besant admitted that Judge had not been guilty of any forgery. It is somehow odd that in most of the present-day lodges, Besant is seen as the figurehead of the Theosophical Society, at the expense of Blavatsky. The former had none of the dynamism of her predecessor, and one cannot imagine Blavatsky's will being swayed by Leadbeater, or indeed anyone else.

By Besant and Leadbeater reducing the significance of discrediting the Masters, and virtually discrediting them, the Mahatmas were reduced to nothing more than puppets. Anyone who wished to claim and broadcast their communications could do so. Besant's ploy, to remove their influence, and thus Blavatsky's, from the Theosophical Society almost succeeded. In India, Besant actively promoted the Hindu cause, favouring it in favour of Buddhism, a blatant reversal of Blavatsky and Olcott's support of the Buddhists in Ceylon (Sri Lanka). She joined the Indian National Congress, and as a result of her being involved in an agitation for self-rule in 1917 she was arrested. She was released to much acclaim, but was reduced to being a bit-player when, a year later, Ghandi became the leading figure in the movement. Besant unhappy with the emerging socialist policies withdrew from having an active presence in India.

At the death of Judge, Katherine Augusta Tingley became the new head of the American organisation, although her identity was kept a secret throughout 1897. One wonders why, presumably because her appointment might not have proved universally popular. Tingley seems an amiable if not particularly dynamic character. She wrote several books on Theosophy and related subjects, and embraced the notion of the magical imagination to a degree that might have been unacceptable to Blavatsky. She was certain that, 'the mind properly guided by this power will elevate us all', and if the imagination is permitted to 'soar in the world of spiritual and creative thought...it can create what truly seem to be miraculous things.' [70]

Tingley's powers appear to have impressed no less a person than Aleister Crowley, as he made an attempt to recruit her for his magical organisation the O.T.O. Crowley had proudly informed Tingley that he was born in the year that the Theosophical Society was founded and attempted to draw a comparison between its philosophy and his own. He announced that both he and Blavatsky rejected the Devil's existence and were in accord in rejecting Darwin's scientific materialism. Tingley appears not to have commanded such acclaim among the ranks of the Society, however, as in the following year a group led by Ernest Temple Hargrove seceded from Tingley's organisation and formed a rival group in New York. Tingley's reaction was to transfer the Society's international headquarters to Pasadena, California, where it remains to this day.

In May 1913 Mabel Collins met with Rudolf Steiner, who had recently left the Theosophical Society, and embraced his researches. She later formed the Light on the Path lodge with D.N. Dunlop, a friend of W.B.Yeats. Dunlop was a prominent member of the Theosophical Society in Ireland. Collins died in 1927. The number of those, like her, who had been at the birth of the Theosophical Society had inevitably dwindled. Blavatsky's star had waned, but it was to shine briefly once more at the behest of Alice Bailey, a name that has lasted until the present day in esoteric circles. In 1919 this lady was working as a cook at the New York Lodge of the Theosophical Society. The dramatic advent of a communication from Djwhal Khul led to her writing twenty-four books inspired by the Master. Her second husband Foster Bailey later became National Secretary of the Theosophical Society. Both he and Alice were increasingly at odds with Besant over the latter's 'neo-theosophy'. The Baileys, led the 'Back to Blavatsky' movement within the Society, but their campaign floundered and she and her husband were dismissed from the Society.

It may have been Blavatsky who T.S. Eliot had in mind when he mentions 'Madame Sosotris and her wicked pack of cards' in *The Waste Land*. Certainly the public perception of Blavatsky was as a combination of sorceress and fairground fortune teller. She suffered, as all innovators, and those with a touch of genius, by being ridiculed and vilified. In any other calling she might have fared better, but because she was destined to carry the torch of enlightenment, there were many who ignored the light and preferred to remain where they were – in darkness. As always, the ignorant and the beastly sought to remove her influence from Victorian society, and they did what they could to achieve this end. It is a tribute to Blavatsky's tenacity that they did not succeed, though her struggles took their toll. One would like to believe that she really did adopt the attitude that G.R. Mead her secretary assures us she did, 'Abuse she is accustomed to; calumny she is daily acquainted with; at slander she smiles in silent contempt.' [71]

Certainly Blavatsky had her vices, who does not? One could mention her bad temper, her arrogance or her domineering ways, but this is a small price to pay for her greatness. A disparity often exists between the higher and lower selves of some of the greatest occultists, Eliphas Levi, Aleister Crowley, W.G. Gray and Dion Fortune all had less attractive sides to their nature. One is also aware that much of the time Blavatsky must have thought she was howling in the wilderness, as she struggled to convince dull minds of the existence of a spiritual element in their lives. Whose patience would not have worn thin forced, as she was, to endure so many ill-natured attacks.

The spiritual chain that Blavatsky forged has seen more links added over the decades. The 1960s saw the first glimmerings of a movement that embraced the transcendental, and the twenty-first century has seen an increase of popular interest in higher things. This was Blavatsky's great vision, that mankind would realise that the materialist way was not the path to fulfilment, and in this she was proved correct. It must be said that the determination of an oppressive commercialism to undermine such lofty ideals also exists, so the spiritual vision still firmly remains just that – a vision. Symbols and images, however, do have a habit of making their presence felt...ask any magician!

Without Blavatsky, we should have no 'New Age'. It is unlikely that without her there would have been The Golden Dawn or The Society of Inner Light, or a whole collection of occult organisations that sprang up in their wake. Respected figures in occult circles in the twentieth century may never have involved themselves so wholeheartedly in their studies. Research into esoteric matters, the following of a spiritual path, the study and practice of magic – it is doubtful if any of these would exist. This should be kept in the forefront when any assessment of Blavatsky is being made. Is the name of Hodgson, the investigator sent to India by the society, remembered even for an instant? Do the names of her critics resound in our ears? The answer to these questions, and many others that could be posited, is an emphatic 'No'. We do the memory of Blavatsky an injustice if we do not recognise her worth, and if we dismiss the fortitude which she continually displayed, then we are not worthy of the presence of such a colossus, such a Lion of Light.

Astrological Analysis

In *The Secret Doctrine*, Blavatsky expounds briefly on the subject of astrology. As we are about to embark upon an analysis of her character using this science, it would seem only fair to quote her assessment of its origin and purpose:

> As above, so below. Sidereal phenomena, and the behaviour of the celestial bodies in the heavens were taken as a model, and the plan was carried out blow on Earth. In the same manner and on the plan of the zodiac in the Upper Ocean or the heavens, a certain realm on Earth, an inland sea, was consecrated and called the 'Abyss of learning', twelve centres on it in the shape of twelve small islands...[72]

Consciously or not, the above may be a reference to the 'Glastonbury Zodiac' a group of twelve features in the Somerset landscape, each one of which represents a sign of the zodiac. The basic premise of astrology is that at any moment, the celestial bodies are aligned in such a way as to have a particular effect upon an event talking place on the earthly plane.

Modern technology has ensured that the data of time and place of birth can be converted into a 'birth chart' instantaneously. However, the interpretation of a nativity, the 'zodiacal map' that is drawn, is not part of physical science it is still an art. The writer has forty years of experience with astrology, and this combined with insights from other respected astrologers has produced extremely interesting results, ones which give further insights into Blavatsky's character.

Blavatsky has her sun in Leo, moon in Libra and Cancer on the ascendant. Apart from the ascendant, which is in a Water sign, she has no planet in a sign of this element. Psychic ability is generally associated with this element, but in Blavatsky's case it is indicated by the presence of planets in the 'psychic' houses, the Fourth, and particularly the Eighth. Blavatsky has Venus conjunct the Moon, in the Fourth House, and Jupiter conjunct Uranus in the Eighth House. The latter aspect is particularly strong, as Uranus is the planet of magic and Jupiter always enhances any other planet with which it is in aspect. Blavatsky's universal philosophy and great vision for mankind is contained here. Uranus is in Aquarius, that sign being ruled by this planet, and thus making the magical vibration even more potent. The Moon is in trine with these two planets thus enhancing the unconscious ability to create phenomena.

As the sun is in opposition to Uranus and Jupiter, there would be a likelihood of difficulties in fully manifesting this power. In Blavatsky's case this was the opposition to her cause that she faced in her life, and the deceit she encountered, as shown in the position of Neptune, the planet of deception in the Seventh House, the area of personal relationships. That she attracted those who meant her no good is also apparent in the opposition between Neptune in Capricorn and her ascendant Cancer. The nebulous quality of Neptune made her susceptible to drugs, and these created a sense of unreality that she found difficult not to indulge in. This denial of the truth led her to assume much that was inaccurate concerning her acquaintances. Quarrels too were periodically a feature of Blavatsky's life, and this is indicated in the Mars and Saturn conjunction in the Third House, the area of communications with acquaintances and siblings. These so called 'malefic' planets exert their influence is an egocentric and assertive way. As they are placed in the sign of Virgo, a tendency to criticise and find fault with those around her was a character-istic of Blavatsky.

The placing of Mars and Saturn is also responsible for the compulsive tendency to write which Blavatsky owned. This writer, having the same placing of these two planets in his own nativity, is able to personally vouch for this obsession. It also bestows a desire to communicate on any level, which is why Blavatsky could hold sway in any company with her conversation. A dangerous aspect of this placing is a threat to the health, particularly from smoking. The Third House traditionally rules that part of the body which includes the chest and Blavatsky would have been well-advised to refrain from this habit, which she stubbornly refused to do. There is more than a hint of a masculine side to her character reflected, among other traits, in her adopting the then exclusively male habit of smoking.

Much astrological activity centres on the Houses already mentioned, and these are the two key areas of the chart. Mention should also be made of the Second House in which the sun and Pluto in conjunction are placed. The implication here, as Pluto is acknowledged in the modern system as the ruler of the Eighth House, is of a strengthening of those areas. Specifically we are dealing with Blavatsky's affinity with the otherworld, in the sense of past lives and reincarnation. It is from this rooted attachment to the past that the essence of the Masters derives. Blavatsky was more than 'in touch' with spirits of the past and the aether, she was part of that mysterious milieu. The significance of the Second House in this placing, is the manner in which Blavatsky had some monetary gain from her occultism, yet the rewards were equalled by the sufferings that she endured. A karmic payback is in operation here without doubt.

The Fourth House also needs consideration, for that is the area of life concerned with the mother, both biological and in terms of the maternal instinct. Blavatsky was affectionate and loyal to those whom she was close yet reserved her deepest affections for the Masters and Theosophy. She may have entertained a desire to mother the world, not in the sense of an 'earth mother', but more of a spiritual maternity. Blavatsky did feel a particular affinity with Isis, and was convinced that she herself lived beyond the Veil. Her insisting upon an environment where she could display the things that had sentiment for her, as well as creating a grand affect was due to the influence of Leo and Libra in her chart. She introduced a feminine aspect to the spiritual at the time when the organisations that were available to women were dominated by men. She dressed in a regal manner, rather as one would expect from someone from her privileged background.

Blavatsky had no use for constraints, as shown by the rejection of her first partner after her first marriage, this desire for independence and innovation came from the hard aspects between the sun and Uranus. Her embracing of another culture, the difficulties she had with being able to communicate in the language of that culture are emphasised in the aspects between Mercury and Saturn. She must have felt a sense of frustration engendered by her lack of any formal education, particularly when she came to write her books. The self-discipline necessary for such a task is there, and the sense of being chosen for the task is also present.

Her health concerns are also highlighted, particularly in those areas of how the body eliminates waste, and the function of the sexual organs. Blavatsky suffered from Bright's Disease, which affects the kidneys. She was also burdened emotionally and physically in her inability to fulfil her sexual desires.

References

1. William Kingsland, *The real H.P. Blavatsky – A study in Theosophy, and a memoir of a Great Soul.* (London: Theosophical Publishing House 1928)
2. A.P. Sinnett, *Incidents in the life of Madame Blavatsky* (London Theosophical Publishing House 1913)
3. *ibid.*
4. Daniel Nicol Dunlop, Interview with Mr. W.B. Yeats (The Irish Theosophist – (Dublin, Ireland) November 15, 1893, pp. 147-149.
5. In Memory of Helena Petrovna Blavatsky by Some of her Pupils (London: Theosophical Publishing Society 1891)
6. H.P. Blavatsky, A.T. Barker, *Letters of H.P. Blavatsky to A.P. Sinnett* (London: Kessinger Publishing, 2003)
7. Jane Robinson, *Unsuitable for Ladies – An Anthology of Women Travellers* (Oxford: Oxford University Press 1994)
8. Sinnett ibid.
9. Col. H.S. Olcott, *Old Diary Leaves 1875-8 – The True Story of The Theosophical Society* (Cambridge; University Press 2011)
10. Col. H.S.Olcott, *People from the other World* (1874)
11. Sinnett *ibid.*
12. Sinnett *ibid.*
13. Later published by the Theosophical Society as a pamphlet.
14. Olcott *ibid.*
15. Joseph Campbell, *The Hero with a Thousand Faces,* (London: Fontana 1993)
16. H.S. Olcott, *Buddhist Catechism* REF
17. Campbell *ibid.*
18. H.P. Blavatsky Collected Writings Vol. IV
19. Mary Lutyens, *The Years of Awakening* (London: John Murray 1975)
20. *A Primer of Theosophy* (Chicago Ill : The Rajput Press 1909)

21. *ibid.*
22. William Kingsland, *The Real H.P. Blavatsky – A Study in Theosophy, and a memoir of a great soul* (London: Theosophical Publishing House 1928)
23. J. Hamill, *The Rosicrucian Seer: The magical writings of Frederick Hockley* (Wellingborough: The Aquarian Press 1986)
24. Alexander Wilder M.D., 'How Isis Unveiled Was Written', *The Word* May 1908 (7:2)
25. *ibid.*
26. H.P.Blavatsky, *Isis Unveiled* (London: Theosophical Publishing House 1932)
27. *ibid.*
28. *ibid.*
29. Olcott *ibid*
30. John Symonds, *In the Astral Light – The Life of Madame Blavatsky – Medium and Magician* (London: Odhams Press 1959)
31. Symonds *ibid.*
32. Elizabeth Preston, Christmas Humphreys (eds), *An Abridgment of the Secret Doctrine* (London : Theosophical Publishing House 1966)
33. Maurice Maeterlinck, *The Great Secret* (London: Bibliobazaar 2009)
34. Adolph Franck, (trans. I Sossnitz), *The Kabbalah – The Religious Philosophy of the Hebrews* (New York: Arno Press 1973)
35. *ibid.*
36. Symonds *ibid*
37. Sinnet *ibid*
38. VsevolodSergyeevichSolovyoff, *A Modern Priestess of Isis* (London, Longmans, Green:1895)
39. Godfrey Higgins, *Anacalypsis: An Attempt to Draw Aside the Veil of the Saitic Isis or an Inquiry into the Origin of Languages, Nations and Religions)* (London: University Books 1965)

40. *ibid.*

41. *ibid*

42. H.P. Blavatsky, *The Key to Theosophy* (Los Angeles 1930)

43. *ibid*

44. Mabel Collins, *The Idyll of the White Lotus* (Adyar, India: Theosophical Publishing House 1933)

45. *ibid*

46. *ibid*

47. *ibid*

48. H.P.Blavatsky, *Nightmare Tales,* (London: Theosophical Publishing House 1895)

49. H.P. Blavatsky, *The Sound of Silence* (London: Theosophical Publishing House 1895)

50. Colin Wilson, *Aleister Crowley, The Nature of the Beast* (London: Harrap 1887)

51. Blavatsky, *Isis Unveiled*

52. A.P. Sinnett. *The Occult World*

53. Rene Guenon, *Le Theosophisme – histoire d'une pseudo-religion* (1921)

54. Dr. Vernon Harrison *J'accuse – An examination of the Hodgson Report of 1885.* (Pasadena U.S.A. Theosophical University Press 1986, 1997)

55. A.P. Sinnett, *Incidents in the life of Madame Blavatsky* (London: Theosophical Publishing House 1913)

56. Eliphas Levi, (trans. A.E.Waite), *Dogme et rituel de la Haute Magie* (1910)

57. Blavatsky *Key to Theosophy. ibid*

58. Maria Carlson, *No Religion Higher than Truth – A History of the Theosophical Movement in Russia 1875 -1922* (Princeton: Princeton University Press 1951)

59. H.P. Blavatsky, A.T.Barker *Letters of H.P.Blavatsky to A.P.Sinnett* (London: Kessinger Publishing, 2003)

60. Beatrice Hastings, *A Defence of Madame Blavatsky* (1937) Pamphlet.

61. Blavatsky *Isis Unveiled ibid.*
62. Harrison *ibid*
63. Symonds *ibid*
64. Harrison, *ibid.*
65. John Tyndall, *Fragments of Science For Unscientific People: A Series of Detached Essays, Lectures, and Reviews.* (University of Michigan Library 2006)
66. Ivor Grattan Guinness (ed,) *Psychical Research – A Guide to its history and practices. – In celebration of 100years of the Society for Psychical Research* (Wellingborough: The Aquarian Press 1982)
67. *In Memory of Helena Petrovna Blavatsky by Some of her Pupils,*(London: Theosophical Publishing Society 1891)
68. Edward Maitland, *Anna Kingsford, Her Life, Letters, Diary and Work* (London: George Redway, 1896).
69. United Lodge of Theosophists, *The Theosophical Movement, 1875- 1950* (Los Angeles: Cunningham Press 1951) p. 351
70. Blavatsky *Isis Unveiled ibid.*
71. GRS Mead(Pamphlet) (Theosophical Publishing House, Adyar, Madras, India, 1920.
72. Blavatsky *The Secret Doctrine ibid.*

Bibliography

Barborka, Geoffrey A., *H.P. Blavatsky, Tibet and Tulku* (Adyar, India Theosophical Publishing House 1966)

Blavatsky, H.P., *An Abridgement of the Secret Doctrine* (edited Elizabeth Preston, Christmas Humphreys) (London: Theosophical Publishing House 1966)

Blavatsky, H.P., *Practical Occultism* (Illinois: Theosophical Press 1937)

Blavatsky, H.P., *The Voice of Silence* (Adyar, India Theosophical)

Blavatsky, H.P., *The Secret Doctrine: the Synthesis of Science, Religion, and Philosophy*: (Cambridge University Press 2011)

Blavatsky H.P., *Isis Unveiled* Secret of the Ancient Wisdom Tradition (N.Y: Quest Books 1997)

Collins, Mabel, *The Idyll of the White Lotus* (Adyar, India: Theosophical Publishing House 1933)

De Zirkoff, Boris, *Rebirth of the Occult Tradition – How the Secret Doctrine of H.P.Blavatsky was written.* (London: Theosophical Publishing House 1977)

Franck, Adolph, *The Kabbalah – The Religious Philosophy of the Hebrews* (trans. I Sossnitz) (New York: Arno Press 1973)

Grattan-Guiness, Ivor (Ed) *Psychical Research – A guide to its history, principles and Practices. – In Celebration of 100 years of the Society for Psychical Research.* (Wellingborough; The Aquarian Press 1982)

Greer, Mary K., *Women of the Golden Dawn – Rebels and Priestesses* (Rochester, Illinois: Park Street Press 1995)

Kingsford, Anna *The Perfect Way, or The Finding of Christ* (London: Bibliobazaar 2009)

Kingsland, William, *The Real H.P. Blavatsky – A Study in Theosophy, and a memoir of a great soul* (London: Theosophical Publishing House 1928)

Knight, Gareth, *A History of White magic,* (London: Mowbrays

1978)

Neff, Mary K., *Personal memories of H.P. Blavatsky* (Wheaton, Illinois: The Theosophical Publishing House1937)

Robinson, Jane, *Unsuitable for Ladies – An Anthology of Women Travellers* (Oxford: Oxford University Press 1994)

Sinnett, A.P., *Incidents in the life of Madame Blavatsky* (London Theosophical Publishing House 1913)

Sinnett, A.P., *The Mahatma Letters* (Pasadena, California Theosophical University Press 1923)

Sinnett, A.P., *The Occult World* (London: Theosophical Publishing House 1913)

Symonds, John, *In the Astral Light – The Life of Madame Blavatsky – Medium and Magician* (London: Odhams Press 1959)

Tomberg, Valentin, *Meditations on the Tarot* (New York: Element Books 1993)

AXIS MUNDI
BOOKS

Axis Mundi Books provide the most revealing and coherent explorations and investigations of the world of hidden or forbidden knowledge. Take a fascinating journey into the realm of Esoteric Mysteries, Magic, Mysticism, Angels, Cosmology, Alchemy, Gnosticism, Theosophy, Kabbalah, Secret Societies and Religions, Symbolism, Quantum Theory, Apocalyptic Mythology, Holy Grail and Alternative Views of Mainstream Religion.